## Praise for
### *Finding Financial Freedom*

"This is solid financial advice that you can bank on! Grant Jeffrey knows finances and understands how to help you with yours. Don't miss this wise, practical, and helpful guide to building your financial future."

—DR. ED HINDSON, Assistant Chancellor,
Liberty University

"Grant Jeffrey is a conservative financial voice crying out in a liberal financial wasteland. His words bring a fresh, biblical, and pragmatic approach to solving your money problems. The section on achieving financial independence, particularly the part on arranging an investment portfolio, is worth the price of the book."

—NEIL ATKINSON, author of *The Shrewd Christian*

"As usual, Grant Jeffrey's latest work is a masterpiece. He never leaves a stone unturned in his exposition of any subject, and I totally recommend this new volume because of its solid biblical foundation."

—DR. JACK VAN IMPE, president of Jack Van Impe
Ministries International

FINDING

# FINANCIAL
# FREEDOM

# FINDING
# FINANCIAL
# FREEDOM

## A BIBLICAL
## GUIDE
## TO YOUR
## INDEPENDENCE

# GRANT R. JEFFREY, CLU
### BEST-SELLING AUTHOR

WATERBROOK
PRESS

FINDING FINANCIAL FREEDOM
PUBLISHED BY WATERBROOK PRESS
12265 Oracle Blvd., Suite 200
Colorado Springs, Colorado 80921
*A division of Random House, Inc.*

All Scripture quotations are taken from the *King James Version*.

The financial advice in this book is intended to serve as a general guideline. Neither the author nor the publisher is engaged in rendering legal, accounting, or other financial professional services by publishing this book. As each individual situation is unique, questions relevant to personal finances and specific to an individual should be addressed to an appropriate professional.

ISBN 1-4000-7105-4

Library of Congress Cataloging-in-Publication Data
Jeffrey, Grant R.
    Finding financial freedom : the biblical road to wealth / Grant R. Jeffrey. — 1st ed.
        p. cm.
    Includes bibliographical references.
    ISBN 1-4000-7105-4
    1. Finance, Personal. 2. Finance, Personal—Religious aspects—Christianity. I. Title.
    HG179.J34 2005
    332.024'01—dc22

                                    2005011168

Printed in the United States of America

2005—First Edition
10 9 8 7 6 5 4 3 2 1

I dedicate this book to my beloved father, Lyle E. Jeffrey, who went home to heaven on January 19, 2004. My father completed his life of eighty-five years having produced a tremendous spiritual legacy represented by countless lives he touched through personal witnessing, numerous speaking engagements, and the many thousands of young campers who attended Frontier Ranch, our family's western-style camp near Ottawa, Canada.

My father taught me many of the biblically based financial truths and investment principles that are explored in this book. As an entrepreneur, he created Jeffrey Luggage Inc., a successful company that provided the profits to enable my parents to operate Frontier Ranch for twenty-five years. He derived much of his financial and investment sense from the numerous scriptural passages that deal with the vital role of money in this life. He taught me that the value of money is as a tool to accomplish our goals and assist others.

In one of our last conversations, Dad spoke of a key verse in the book of Proverbs that he and my mother often quoted. This verse holds what has become a guiding principle in my family's financial life: "Trust in the LORD with all thine heart; and lean not unto thine own understanding. In all thy ways acknowledge him, and he shall direct thy paths" (3:5–6).

# CONTENTS

# ACKNOWLEDGMENTS

*Finding Financial Freedom* is the result of many years of research in countless books, articles, magazines, and a variety of financial and investment courses, including the Chartered Life Underwriter degree that I earned from the University of Toronto. The practical strategies and advice in the following chapters are heavily influenced by the thousands of interviews I have conducted with clients in the course of eighteen years as a professional financial planner.

These interviews with professionals, entrepreneurs, and business owners provided deep insights into the role of setting and establishing sound saving and investment habits, as well as the need for lifetime study for those who wish to achieve and maintain financial independence.

Over the last four decades, I have benefited enormously from the financial and investment advice provided by investment counselors such as the late Larry Burkett, Ron Blue, David Ramsey, and Suze Orman. The valued sources of financial information and wisdom also include Strategic Investment, the Oxford Group, Agora Group, and the *McAlvany Intelligence Advisor*.

A special thanks to my beloved wife, Kaye, for her financial wisdom and business skills that made Frontier Research Publications Inc. successful.

# Finding Financial Freedom

*When I chased after money, I never had enough.*
*When I got my life on purpose and focused on*
*giving of myself and everything that arrived*
*into my life, then I was prosperous.*
—WAYNE DYER

Don't underestimate the power and impact of your financial decisions. Few choices that you make in life will affect your success—or your failure—as much as the decisions you make about your finances. If you fail to manage your financial life wisely, many other areas of life—including your marriage, your other relationships, and your overall happiness—will suffer. There is no area of life, other than your marriage and your relationship with God, that is more vital to your overall success and happiness.

Many studies of marriage and divorce have revealed that financial difficulties are the number one cause of marital breakdown. Financial problems are also a major cause of distress for those who are single. And tragically, a tremendous number of people graduate from high school and college with virtually no meaningful education in how to handle their money. They are unprepared to achieve the goal of being financially independent by the time they retire. Very few have received even a minimum financial education on setting a budget, balancing a checkbook, acquiring a home, evaluating a mortgage offer, comparing credit-card offers, weighing investment alternatives, determining insurance needs and the value of a will, and retirement planning.

Most people, however, have the goal of achieving financial freedom—usually defined as an amount of guaranteed income generated from your investments sufficient to meet your family's income needs for the foreseeable future. You will not automatically become a better or happier person if you achieve financial success. However, you will certainly have many more options available to fulfill your goals for yourself and your family, as well as the opportunity to assist others, including helping the church to reach out to those in need and share the gospel with them. My wife, Kaye, and I have met many individuals who have achieved financial independence and have then embarked on a second career in volunteer work or world missions. One of the greatest benefits of achieving financial freedom is that you will have the opportunity to assist those around you, because you will have extra assets beyond your family's needs. While financial success will not lead to happiness, it can provide a peace of mind that will enable you to focus on other important areas in your family's life.

Unfortunately, too many people never stop to consider or pray about the type and quality of life they wish to pursue. Instead of making thoughtful decisions, they simply drift through life waiting for God to "open or close a door" to let them know how to make the most critical decisions. This is a tragedy, because the major decisions we make will determine the course and quality of the rest of our lives. God promises to give wisdom to anyone who sincerely asks Him for guidance, and we need to learn how to discern the wisdom of God concerning our major decisions.

## THE BENEFITS OF FINANCIAL INDEPENDENCE

Financial freedom and financial independence—how could achieving these goals affect the rest of your life? What would you do if you had a guaranteed income for you and your family so that you no longer were required to work every day? Imagine what you would do if you were truly free! Would you take a one-year sabbatical with your spouse to travel and assist in worldwide missions? Would you finally take that trip to Europe or Asia to explore the wonders of our diverse world? What would you do if you were finally free to follow your heart's desire? Who would you help if you had the resources to make a difference?

There are three major decisions that will impact the rest of your life: Whom will you live your life for? Whom will you live your life with? What will you live your life in?

1. Whom will you live your life for? Will you live for yourself as your own "god"? Or will you choose to accept that your life is not really your own but rather that it belongs to God? The decision to submit your will to faith in Jesus Christ as your Lord and God will transform your life and your purpose forever. This is the most important decision you will ever make, because it will determine your eternal destination, and it will also play a major role in every other decision in your life.

2. Whom will you live your life with? Far too many people marry the person they happen to be dating when the rest of their friends start deciding to marry. Your choice of a wife or husband as your lifetime companion will have a profound effect on every other area and decision of your life. It is vital that you wisely choose God's will for your life companion.

3. What will you live your life in? Your choice of a career in a particular business or profession will have a tremendous impact on every other element of your life. Too many people spend their working years in a business

or profession simply because that was their first job or because a relative influenced their decision. We need to seriously pray for God's wisdom and guidance in this vital life decision.

The income that covers your daily expenses is produced either from your labor or from capital you have invested. Initially we work for money so that money can ultimately work for us. Either a person will continue working to produce an income to provide for his daily needs, or he must accumulate an amount of money (capital) that will produce an income stream to provide for his needs through the retirement years.

It is tragic that the average North American citizen, after working a lifetime in the most prosperous society in history, will retire with far less income and assets than he will need to support a comfortable lifestyle. The problem isn't that people plan to fail; it's that people fail to plan. My hope is that the principles and knowledge presented in this book will enable you and your family to achieve financial freedom.

## FINANCIAL IGNORANCE

By the time the average adult begins a career, he has invested between twelve and sixteen years in formal education. The average student will complete more than fifteen thousand hours of study in a great variety of subjects. However, the vast majority will graduate without a single hour of financial instruction on the practical facts of life needed to achieve financial success. Millions of Americans graduate from high school without receiving practical information on banking, mortgages, credit cards, home ownership, insurance, and wills.

The Charles Schwab Foundation conducted a fascinating study on typical American teenagers' financial knowledge. The study revealed an amazing level of ignorance in young people as they began their careers. The study discovered that "one in five American teenagers doesn't know that if you take out a loan, you must pay it back with interest. One in four thinks that financial aid will pay for all college expenses. And one in three thinks monthly Social Security payments will be all they need to retire."[1]

One study indicated that up to 40 percent of Americans believe that the best chance they have to accumulate $500,000 for their retirement is to win the lottery.[2] When you consider that the likelihood of winning half a million dollars in the lottery is far less than your chance of being hit by lightning—less than one in ten million—you realize there is a serious need for people to become realistic about planning and investing for their retirement.

## QUALITIES THAT TEND TO LEAD TO FINANCIAL INDEPENDENCE

Thomas J. Stanley in his book *The Millionaire Mind* published an intriguing study on the attitudes and characteristics of a number of people who are multimillionaires. Based on in-depth interviews with numerous millionaires, the study found these factors were vital in their financial success:

- Integrity—honesty in all relationships
- Discipline—using self-control in every area of life
- Social skills—friendly relations with people
- A supportive spouse
- Hard work—a willingness to work harder than most people[3]

In his comprehensive study, Stanley discovered that those who achieved true financial independence lived substantially different lives from those who had a high income, high consumption lifestyle that was dependent on credit. For example, more than 90 percent of those who had achieved financial success without acquiring huge debt lived in traditional families with several children and a marriage lasting many decades. Less than 10 percent had inherited a significant part of their wealth. Ninety-seven percent of those surveyed owned their own high-value homes and generally had relatively small mortgages (7 percent of the house's value, on average).

Most millionaires in this group (53 percent) had not moved to a new home in the last ten years.

It is interesting that although they admitted to working hard at a vocation they loved, they stated that spending quality time with family and friends was a significant commitment. Almost one in three of the millionaires owned his own business. Finally, 37 percent of those interviewed stated that their religious faith was a significant influence in their life and their economic success.[4]

Overall, the most significant factor that separates those who achieve financial independence from those who live high income, high consumption, high debt lifestyles is their attitude toward debt and their use of credit. While the high-net-worth millionaires were happy to use credit for their home mortgage and business loans, they generally avoided consumer credit, waiting until they could buy depreciating items such as cars, electronics, and appliances with cash.

I believe that financial bondage to debt leads to spiritual bondage as well: "The borrower is servant to the lender" (Proverbs 22:7). Furthermore, I believe that financial freedom leads to spiritual freedom. To begin the life-long process of achieving financial independence, you need to understand the biblical principles that will guide you through the difficult decisions we all confront in the stages of life. If you are married, you need to discuss with your spouse your finances, goals, and plans. Honestly assess exactly where you are today in income, assets, debts, and net worth. You must first get hold of your debt and credit decisions before you can move toward investment success.

In our materialistic culture, far too many people spend their lives buying products they don't need with money they don't have to impress people they don't like. It's not what you earn that results in your ultimate financial success; it's what you manage to keep and invest that will enable you to build up your assets to achieve financial independence.

Most North Americans will earn well over $2 million in the course of their employable years (between ages twenty and sixty-five). However, the vast majority will retire around age sixty-five with very few personal financial assets beyond their company pension plan and their Social Security payments.

In this book we will examine a variety of investments that can help lead you toward financial independence. In addition, we will look at some of the financial risks that lie ahead, including the dangers of lost income from disability and premature death. We will explore various tools you can use to protect your goal of financial freedom, such as insurance, wills, and powers of attorney. Financial success is a journey, not a destination. We will follow a biblically based path that will help you and your family achieve the financial independence that will enable you to have greater success in every other area of your life.

Why should you work and plan to achieve financial independence? The first reason is to escape the paycheck-to-paycheck lifestyle and financial bondage that oppress most Americans. The second reason is to allow you and your family the financial freedom to enjoy the lifestyle you desire, to pursue educational opportunities for yourself and your children, and to enjoy quality leisure time with your family and friends. Finally, financial success will allow you the pleasure of giving significant funds to assist your church and favorite charities, as well as friends and family who would benefit from wise financial assistance. Giving wisely to others is a great challenge as well as a great joy.

Part 1

# YOU CAN ACHIEVE FINANCIAL FREEDOM

# Chapter 1

# Biblical Principles for Financial Success

## *The Attitudes That Lead to Financial Freedom*

> *Where I was brought up we never talked about*
> *money because there was never enough*
> *to furnish a topic of conversation.*
> —MARK TWAIN

Many people of faith are ambivalent toward the need for financial planning, with most Christians tending to downplay the importance of money. Christians often assure one another that "money isn't everything" and that "money can't buy happiness."

But there are exceptions. Some people focus so exclusively on their finances that they have almost made their financial prosperity the sole measure of whether God is blessing their lives. Clearly, there is a need for balance.

Christians need to develop a biblically based attitude about finances. Obviously, money is important because it affects the quality of our family's life and the opportunities available to those we love. However, we need to recognize that financial resources—including our salary and our assets—are simply tools that the Lord has placed in our hands as a trust to be administered. Someday we will give the Lord an accounting of our stewardship of the finances He has entrusted to us.

## INCORRECT ATTITUDES TOWARD MONEY

Many Christians have never seriously evaluated their attitude toward money and financial planning in light of the principles found in the Word of God. As a consequence, they often possess erroneous and even harmful attitudes that hinder their financial success and peace of mind. Here are four of the most destructive attitudes toward money.

### 1. Money Is Purely Worldly

Some have suggested that those who are truly spiritual should not be concerned with worldly matters, such as our finances. Many believe the Lord is unconcerned with mundane matters such as money, investing, and financial planning. Nothing could be further from the truth. Money is such an important part of our daily lives that God has given us instructions throughout His Word concerning our finances. The Bible provides detailed instructions on how a believer should handle his money, as well as warnings about financial pitfalls that we should avoid.

### 2. Money Is Separate from Our Spiritual Lives

Some believe that their spiritual life is disconnected from "worldly" matters, such as money. They have created an artificial division between the sacred life and the earthly. Some say, "This 10 percent of my money belongs solely to God, but the other 90 percent belongs to me to spend in any way I please." They believe it is somehow fanatical or extreme to involve God in every area of their finances. However, *everything* we have belongs to God. All we now possess or will ever own is simply given in trust to us by the Lord. We are to use our finances according to the balanced principles taught in the Scriptures.

### 3. Financial Success Is Unspiritual

Some suggest that financial success is incompatible with a true spiritual life. They believe that prosperity is suspect and that the poor are inherently more spiritual than the prosperous. Many believe that Christians who succeed financially reached that point by making money their god.

Curiously, the truth is almost exactly the opposite. As a result of thousands of interviews with my clients over two decades as a professional financial planner, I have found that those who are in deep financial trouble actually spend far more time each day thinking about money than those who have achieved a measure of financial success. Once Christians have achieved financial stability and are on the road to financial independence, they can focus on far more important things than worrying about how they will pay their bills. Achieving financial success can be

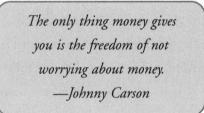

*The only thing money gives you is the freedom of not worrying about money.*
*—Johnny Carson*

spiritually liberating, enabling you to focus on the spiritual goals in your life. Note the biblical figures who were financially prosperous. There were many prosperous Christians in the early church, including Nicodemus and Joseph of Arimathea. And almost all of the Old Testament leaders— including Abraham, Isaac, Jacob, and Job—prospered and used their wealth wisely.

### 4. Financial Planning Indicates a Lack of Trust

Some believe that we should leave it all to God by refusing to plan financially or to set goals. Many spiritualize this passivity to justify their lack of financial discipline. They claim that if God wants them to succeed, they will wake up one day and find they have supernaturally acquired financial independence. Obviously, the Bible does not support the idea of passively awaiting a financial miracle. The Lord commands us to work and plan in order to provide for our families' needs.

## A Biblical Attitude Toward Money

In the area of finances, the attitudes of man and God often differ markedly. While man's attitudes are usually self-centered, the Lord calls on us to base our lives on eternal values in light of our future life in heaven. In the words of Jesus, "For what is a man profited, if he shall gain the whole world, and lose his own soul? or what shall a man give in exchange for his soul?" (Matthew 16:26). As an example of these profound differences, while the Lord tells us, "It is more blessed to give than to receive" (Acts 20:35), most people live as if it is more blessed to receive than to give. God tells us, however, that those who sacrifice for Him in this life shall "receive an hundredfold now in this time…and in the world to come eternal life" (Mark 10:30).

In the parable of the rich man and the beggar, the Lord taught that those whose sole desire is to accumulate riches will ultimately lose everything they value. In contrast, our materialistic age encourages people to measure their value and that of others solely on their ability to make money or acquire investments and possessions. During a trip to California, Kaye and I noted a bumper sticker that summed up this cynical and empty philosophy: "Whoever dies with the most toys wins!" In contrast, the Word of God reminds us that "a man's life consisteth not in the abundance of the things which he possesseth" (Luke 12:15).

We need to evaluate our attitudes toward our finances, investments, and possessions in light of the teachings of the Word of God. Are we truly the owners of the property and money that pass through our hands? Or instead are we stewards who have been entrusted to administer these possessions for the true owner, God, who will someday demand from each of us a full accounting? For Christians, the answer is clear. All we own today and all that we will ever possess in this world should be held lightly, because our possessions are not our own. The Lord commands us, "Lay not up for yourselves treasures upon earth, where moth and rust doth corrupt, and where thieves break through and steal: But lay up for yourselves treasures in heaven, where neither moth nor rust doth corrupt, and where thieves do not break through nor steal" (Matthew 6:19–20).

When we examine the Scriptures, we discover a number of biblical principles that should guide us regarding our financial strategies, principles, goals, and plans. As in every area of life, we need to find the biblically balanced position based on "all the counsel of God" (Acts 20:27).

### God Will Supply Our Needs

My God shall supply all your need according to his riches in glory by Christ Jesus. (Philippians 4:19)

One of the most fundamental biblical truths is that God is vitally concerned with the practical, daily economic needs of faithful followers who trust in Him. Within the pages of Scripture, we find a complete set of principles that should form the foundation of our basic financial strategies during years of prosperity as well as difficult economic times. While Christians await the return of the Lord, we must realize that if He tarries for a number of years, we may likely have to live through an economic roller coaster. Therefore, we need to understand that our ultimate financial source is not our salary or our investments but rather our Father in heaven.

If we ask the Lord, He will guide us with practical financial strategies through His Word and through His Holy Spirit. He will show us what we

need to do to protect our families, our businesses, our churches, and ourselves in the difficult days that may lie ahead. King David described God's
unchanging faithfulness and loving care for His children: "I have been
young, and now am old; yet have I not seen the righteous forsaken, nor his
seed begging bread" (Psalm 37:25). This affirmation from King David confirms God's promised care for those in need who appeal to Him.

### God Commands Diligence and Hard Work

> Be thou diligent to know the state of thy flocks, and look well to
> thy herds. (Proverbs 27:23)

Throughout the Scriptures, God commands us to be diligent in handling
our business affairs and our finances. Note that you cannot find a single
biblical hero or "man of God" who is weak, indecisive, or lazy. While it is
God who prospers our efforts, He expects us to do our part. In Proverbs
we find a number of passages that describe this principle of financial
accountability. The Scriptures promise God's blessing if we diligently and
faithfully work to accomplish our task: "He that tilleth his land shall have
plenty of bread" (Proverbs 28:19). The Scriptures also declare, "Be ye
strong therefore, and let not your hands be weak: for your work shall be
rewarded" (2 Chronicles 15:7).

The Word of God commends our diligent efforts to prepare for our
future needs by directing our attention to the prudent actions of the lowly
ant. "Go to the ant, thou sluggard; consider her ways, and be wise: Which
having no guide, overseer, or ruler, provideth her meat in the summer, and
gathereth her food in the harvest" (Proverbs 6:6–8).

Although God has promised to care for us, in the parable of the servants and the talents, the Lord instructs us to invest the financial resources
He places in our hands to achieve the maximum return. In the Lord's

parable, the two faithful servants who invested their master's talents and achieved a positive return were commended by their master and honored for their faithfulness. However, the servant who passively hid his single talent in the ground was severely reprimanded by his master for his laziness and lack of financial stewardship. The master of the unfaithful servant told him, "Thou wicked and slothful servant…: Thou oughtest therefore to have put my money to the exchangers, and then at my coming I should have received mine own with usury. Take therefore the talent from him, and give it unto him which hath ten talents. For unto every one that hath shall be given, and he shall have abundance: but from him that hath not shall be taken away even that which he hath" (Matthew 25:26–29). This parable commands us to be good stewards and also clarifies Christ's teaching on interest and saving money at financial institutions. While God condemns criminally high interest rates, He commends the master who rewarded his faithful and diligent servants for investing the master's money with bankers to gain a good interest return.

### As You Sow, So Shall You Reap

In Christ's parable of the sower and the seed, He taught that the results we achieve are directly related to the seeds we sow and the quality of the soil we choose. Some Christians believe that we should simply pray with faith and expect the Lord to supply our every financial need, whether or not we have acted as good stewards through following biblical principles, diligent work, planning, and investments. However, the Lord expects each of us to work faithfully and to wisely invest the fruits of our labor: "But this I say, He which soweth sparingly shall reap also sparingly; and he which soweth bountifully shall reap also bountifully" (2 Corinthians 9:6). Once we have faithfully and diligently done our part, we can then prayerfully and confidently ask the Lord to bless our efforts and give us wisdom regarding our investments.

## A BIBLICAL ATTITUDE TOWARD POSSESSIONS

### The Law of Giving and Receiving

If we hold on to our possessions too tightly, we will almost certainly lose them. Every possession we have is simply a trust to be administered for the Lord. Those who accept this principle will be open to helping their family, friends, and neighbors through gifts and practical assistance. After more than eighteen years of professional financial planning with clients and almost four decades as an entrepreneur and investor, I find the evidence compelling that those who are generous in their gifts to the Lord and who assist their neighbors will receive abundant blessings from God.

Our Lord promised that those who joyfully give to others will receive in return many times the amount they give: "Give, and it shall be given unto you; good measure, pressed down, and shaken together, and running over" (Luke 6:38). While this is clearly a biblical principle, our motive should be to give in obedience to God's command, not to give in order to get something in return.

### Understanding Money as a Tool

A biblically balanced attitude toward our finances and possessions is vital. Money and possessions are important tools that provide for our practical needs. Unfortunately, we live in the most materialistic society in history. Television and advertising seduce the values of many people to the point where they believe their own happiness and worth depend on their having the latest car, the finest house, and the most stylish designer clothing. We must consciously resist the sinful materialism of our age that would have us make money and possessions our god.

The Word of God teaches: "For the love [lust] of money is the root of all evil: which while some coveted after, they have erred from the faith, and pierced themselves through with many sorrows" (1 Timothy 6:10). The danger lies in the evil of greediness, a sinful desire to focus solely on the accumulation of money. In other words, if we allow ourselves to fall in love with (or to have an unwholesome desire for) money instead of using it as an essential tool of life, then it will corrupt our lives. A balanced view of money as taught throughout the Word of God reveals that our financial security is a gift from God that allows us to bless not only our families, but also our churches and those around us. God repeatedly commended the faithfulness and financial stewardship of Abraham, Isaac, Jacob, King David, King Solomon, and many others. After Job's long trial, the Lord restored Job's huge fortunes (see Job 42:12).

### Knowing Whom You Serve

Each of us must answer this question regarding our finances: whom will you serve? Ultimately, you will choose to serve Jesus Christ as your Lord God, or you will choose to serve yourself. Jesus warned, "No man can serve two masters: for either he will hate the one, and love the other; or else he will hold to the one, and despise the other. Ye cannot serve God and mammon [money]" (Matthew 6:24).

Will we serve Jesus Christ through our diligence and faithful stewardship, or will we allow materialism and lust for money to overtake us and rob us of the true joy of the Lord? We need to handle our possessions and finances faithfully and prayerfully, knowing that we will someday give an accounting to our Lord Jesus Christ for how we handled our financial life, decisions, and priorities.

Further, we must put our trust in God and not in money. The Bible declares that God wants His followers to prosper and enjoy His blessings. The Lord promised Israel great economic blessings if they would obey His commands: "And the LORD shall make thee plenteous in goods, in the fruit of thy body, and in the fruit of thy cattle, and in the fruit of thy ground, in the land which the LORD sware unto thy fathers to give thee. The LORD shall open unto thee his good treasure, the heaven to give the rain unto thy land in his season, and to bless all the work of thine hand: and thou shalt lend unto many nations, and thou shalt not borrow" (Deuteronomy 28:11–12).

We must place our trust in our heavenly Father, prudently follow His principles, and look to God to direct our paths. My parents instilled in me a profound principle that I have tried to follow throughout my life: "Trust in the LORD with all thine heart; and lean not unto thine own understanding. In all thy ways acknowledge him, and he shall direct thy paths" (Proverbs 3:5–6).

## A BIBLICAL ATTITUDE TOWARD OUR FAMILY'S NEEDS

Some Christians avoid serious insurance planning and preparation of their wills because of a mistaken notion that such planning is unnecessary since "God will provide." The Bible's teaching is clear that, as much as possible, we are responsible for protecting our families from financial difficulties stemming from our premature death. If we live in such abject poverty that we are truly unable to protect them, we can safely trust that the Lord will intervene to take care of our families. However, the Lord will hold us accountable if we are able to provide financial protection but refuse to do so.

Wills and insurance policies are financial tools to protect our families in the event of a premature death or a disability that destroys our ability to provide an essential monthly income. Since none of us has a guaranteed lease on life, we need to provide for the possibility that we may not live or work long enough to accumulate sufficient assets to guarantee a monthly income that will support our families. The apostle Paul commanded Christian believers to provide financially for their spouses and children: "But if any provide not for his own, and specially for those of his own house, he hath denied the faith, and is worse than an infidel" (1 Timothy 5:8).

In chapter 9 we will explore how we can best protect our loved ones with a guaranteed income while simultaneously saving money on our insurance and taxes. Preparing separate wills for a husband and wife is an absolute necessity. If you fail to provide legal and financial instruction for the distribution of your estate to your beneficiaries in your will, then the government will redistribute your assets according to its rigid legal formula. In Proverbs we read these approving words about those who faithfully plan and provide for their family's future: "A good man leaveth an inheritance to his children's children" (13:22).

In these uncertain times, it would be easy for Christians to lose their sense of peace under God's protection and surrender to despair over the potential economic upheavals facing our world from threats of terrorism, weapons of mass destruction, stock market disruptions, and inflation. However, as believers in Jesus Christ, we can confidently look to the Lord to protect us.

Since God's nature does not change, we can be confident that the Lord still watches over each of His followers. While this does not guarantee that we will never suffer a devastating accident, illness, or economic loss, we do know that nothing can happen in our lives unless God allows it to occur. Satan acknowledged God's supernatural protection of Job with these words: "Hast not thou made an hedge about him, and about his house, and about all that he hath on every side? Thou hast blessed the work of his hands, and his substance is increased in the land" (Job 1:10). While God expects each of us to be diligent and prudent in our finances, our financial prosperity and economic destiny ultimately lie in His hands.

## A BIBLICAL ATTITUDE TOWARD GENEROSITY

He that giveth unto the poor shall not lack: but he that hideth his eyes shall have many a curse. (Proverbs 28:27)

There is one other vital biblical principle regarding financial success, and that is giving generously to those in need. Our joyful willingness to open our hearts and bank accounts to people in great need, whether through ministries or directly to individuals, will open the blessings of heaven upon our own financial condition. And bear in mind that generous giving to others is not limited to financial gifts that are blessed by the IRS with a tax-deductible receipt.

The Lord specifically commands us to give to others as well as to God's storehouse, His church, if we wish to receive His supernatural blessings from heaven. Jesus taught about the relationship between faithful sowing and reaping in His parables. The apostle Paul also wrote, "But this I say, He which soweth sparingly shall reap also sparingly; and he which soweth bountifully shall reap also bountifully. Every man according as he purposeth in his heart, so let him give; not grudgingly, or of necessity: for God loveth a cheerful giver" (2 Corinthians 9:6–7).

God connects His promise to bless and prosper our financial endeavors directly to our generous giving to the Lord's work and to others in need. The prophet Malachi wrote: "Bring ye all the tithes into the storehouse, that there may be meat in mine house, and prove me now herewith, saith the LORD of hosts, if I will not open you the windows of heaven, and pour you out a blessing, that there shall not be room enough to receive it" (Malachi 3:10). Christians who obediently follow the directions in Scripture to carefully arrange their financial affairs according to godly principles can reasonably expect that God will bless their financial dealings to produce financial independence.

# Chapter 2

# Building a Plan for Financial Freedom

*Success Demands That You Set the Right Goals*

> *If a person gets his attitude toward*
> *money straight, it will help straighten out*
> *almost every other area in his life.*
> —BILLY GRAHAM

From the moment you begin your working life until retirement at age sixty-five, you will earn a considerable fortune—for most Americans, far more than $2 million! The North American economy provides unparalleled opportunities for acquiring investments and wealth that people in past generations could not possibly imagine.

The question is this: what will you do with this astonishing opportunity to achieve financial success?

According to the U.S. Census Bureau, "The real median household income remained unchanged between 2002 and 2003 at $43,318."[1] This means that the average American family will see more than $2 million pass through their hands during their working years. However, the vast majority will fail to arrange their financial affairs to achieve the success that is clearly within their grasp.

Between now and age sixty-five you will earn the following amount:

| YOUR AGE TODAY | YOUR AVERAGE MONTHLY INCOME | | | |
|---|---|---|---|---|
| | $2,000 | $3,000 | $4,000 | $5,000 |
| 20 | $1,080,000 | $1,620,000 | $2,160,000 | $2,700,000 |
| 25 | 960,000 | 1,440,000 | 1,920,000 | 2,400,000 |
| 30 | 840,000 | 1,260,000 | 1,680,000 | 2,100,000 |
| 35 | 720,000 | 1,080,000 | 1,440,000 | 1,800,000 |
| 40 | 600,000 | 900,000 | 1,200,000 | 1,500,000 |
| 45 | 480,000 | 720,000 | 960,000 | 1,200,000 |
| 50 | 360,000 | 540,000 | 720,000 | 900,000 |
| 55 | 240,000 | 360,000 | 480,000 | 600,000 |

These figures reveal the enormous economic resources you have at your disposal during your life. But how much of this fortune will you retain to invest and use to provide income during your retirement? Ultimately, it is not what you earn, but what you save and invest that will produce financial success or failure. If you can discipline yourself to save even 10 percent of your monthly earnings, you can wisely and conservatively invest these funds to achieve true financial independence for yourself and your family.

## YOUR GOAL: FINANCIAL INDEPENDENCE

Financial independence can be defined as accumulating an amount of invested capital that will produce a stream of guaranteed income to meet your financial needs without your having to work to earn a salary. You can achieve this goal if you apply some fundamental and biblical principles of finance and then work consistently toward your goal. In a later chapter we will examine several strategies to build your investments as well as to protect yourself and your family against the financial risks in this new millennium.

The majority of people reach retirement without achieving financial independence because they have failed to plan properly and to consistently invest the tremendous resources that God has placed in their hands. Most people have tried—and failed—to develop a workable budget and savings plan. They cash their paychecks and then pay their bills and living expenses, hoping to tithe to God and to save some money out of whatever is left. With this approach, however, there is seldom any cash left at the end of the month to tithe or save. Many believe the simple solution is to increase their income. However, unless they change their strategy and habits, they will never escape the financial bondage of living paycheck to paycheck.

The only practical solution is to change your saving strategy. The principle is simple but fundamental: When you cash your paycheck, pay God His tithe first. Next, pay yourself by depositing 10 percent of your check into a savings account or another investment vehicle. Then pay your outstanding bills and living expenses out of the remaining 80 percent. If you are now living from paycheck to paycheck, this simple but profound

> *Whatever you have; spend less.*
> *—Samuel Johnson*

change in your saving-and-spending strategy will mark the first step on your long but effective road toward financial success.

You may believe you cannot afford to save 10 percent of your income because you are too deeply in debt. The truth is that you cannot afford to delay starting your savings plan no matter how deeply you are mired in debt. The best way to end your financial and spiritual bondage to debt is to take control of your finances by beginning your new savings strategy today. If you cannot commit to saving 10 percent of your income today, then begin at 5 percent and gradually increase the percentage.

The key is to *begin today.* Will there ever be a better time to take control of your financial destiny? Promise yourself that you will start today to follow a plan that will lead to financial freedom. As you see your savings account grow each month, you will unlock your motivation to succeed. Instead of working just to pay your bills and service your debt, you will begin working for your family's financial freedom.

## YEAR-END ANALYSIS OF YOUR FINANCIAL PROGRESS

As you begin each new year, I strongly suggest you review your goals as well as the previous year's financial results. You and your spouse should ask yourselves three basic questions during your year-end summary:

1. Did we succeed in saving a significant amount of money during the last year?

2. Did we succeed in paying off a significant portion of our debts?

3. How does our current net worth, based on the financial balance sheet, compare with our net worth from the previous year? (Use the sample financial balance sheet at the end of this chapter to calculate your net worth.)

If your answers to these three questions are positive, then you are moving in the right direction. However, if your answers are negative, then you need to make some significant changes in your budget and debt-paying strategy.

Your ability to achieve financial goals is not controlled by outside circumstances. You are the only one who can affect your life in a major way. You can improve your financial future by changing your attitude, goals, and actions. Begin with your attitude, which should be characterized by a strong desire to succeed, a willingness to overcome obstacles, and an ability to continually analyze your plans and their results. Next, begin to take control of your money by setting definite financial goals. These goals should be high enough to motivate you and your spouse, but they must also be realistic enough so you truly believe they are attainable. Finally, follow through by acting on a set of balanced financial strategies based on the Word of God, and take into account a sound analysis of the particular risks and opportunities in today's economy. Ask yourself, "If I achieve the same financial results in the next five years as I have during the past five years, will I be satisfied?" If your answer is no, you need to commit today to changing your financial strategy.

## SETTING GOALS IS VITAL TO FINANCIAL SUCCESS

You will never succeed financially unless you set goals. It has been truthfully said that if you aim at nothing, you are almost sure to achieve it. You need to study your financial options, make decisions, and then invest regularly and wisely. Financial success can be described as the progressive realization over time of your predetermined financial goals. However, numerous studies reveal that most people who fail economically have inadequate and vague financial goals that are not committed to paper.

A major study revealed that 27 percent of Americans have no financial goals at all and usually arrive at retirement with less than $25,000 in net assets and a meager Social Security pension. Sixty percent of people have only the vaguest of financial goals; they will barely survive with modest personal assets of $50,000 plus Social Security. Ten percent of those surveyed have financial goals but never put them in writing. However, even the people who have unwritten goals still accumulate an average of $250,000 by age sixty-five, more than ten times the retirement assets of those who have no goals at all.[2]

A famous Harvard University study discovered that only 3 percent of its 1953 graduates had clearly defined written goals. A follow-up study twenty years later revealed that the 3 percent with written goals had accumulated more than the entire combined wealth of the 97 percent of graduates who did not have written goals.[3] The bottom line is this: if you are not setting financial goals to succeed, then you are effectively planning for financial failure. The choice is yours.

If you are married, it is worthwhile to establish meaningful financial and life goals with your spouse at least annually. Once a year take time to review your actual accomplishments compared to your written goals from twelve months earlier. Every year on New Year's Eve, Kaye and I celebrate another year of publishing and ministry at a favorite restaurant. We bring along the book in which we record our goals and objectives. Over dinner we note our accomplishments of the past year. Then we prayerfully discuss and outline our new goals and objectives for the coming year.

The goals we set every year cover three time intervals and encompass several distinct categories. Our goals are (1) short-term (one year), (2) intermediate (five years), and (3) long-term (ten years). The categories include (a) financial: savings and asset buildup, debt reduction, and income objectives; (b) ministry: a new book, new videos, conferences, foreign mission trips; (c) personal: vacations, education, health, physical exercise; and (d) material: home improvement, car, computer equipment.

Setting goals together and recording our accomplishments as God blesses our endeavors is one of the most satisfying moments of the year. It is an opportunity to thank God for His many blessings and to prayerfully ask the Lord for His direction in our future goals and objectives. This exercise reminds us of the tremendous blessings God has granted us. We all should thank God every day for them and recognize our responsibilities as stewards of the financial resources He has placed in our hands.

## FINANCIAL STRATEGIES FOR ECONOMICALLY UNCERTAIN TIMES

In light of the growing dangers to the economy, the stock and bond markets, and real-estate values due to such factors as terrorism and exploding energy prices, we need to be prudent in our financial plans. Those who are aware of the dangers will be able to protect their homes, their businesses, and their family's financial assets by following a conservative course of action. Consider the following strategies during uncertain times:

1. Reduce your debt and build up your liquid cash as quickly as possible. Use treasury bills, certificates of deposit, and money-market funds to safely store cash until you accumulate at least $5,000, at which point you can begin a serious investment program in a well-researched mutual fund with a positive investment record over the last five years.

2. Avoid weak financial institutions, including weak savings and loans, small banks, insurance companies, and trust companies. Check out your bank's strength by ordering a Weiss or Veribanc Report (at a cost of $15 to $25 per report). These resources are available on the Internet and are listed in the appendix at the end of this book.

3. Choose mutual funds that have demonstrated a strong track record over the last five to ten years. Check the performance of various mutual funds on Internet financial sites.

4. Avoid investing in corporate and rental real estate in light of warnings about a growing real-estate bubble.

5. Take advantage of your home as an excellent long-term investment. Prepaying your home mortgage is one of the best financial strategies you can follow. Chapter 6 demonstrates the tremendous financial returns from paying off your mortgage quickly.

6. Avoid corporate bonds, commodities, and other complex, high-risk derivative investments that are difficult for the average investor to evaluate

properly. The risk clearly outweighs the potential gain for all except professional investors.

7. Make limited use of government bonds, treasury bills, certificates of deposit, and fixed-term deposits. These instruments are insured by the federal government and provide a guaranteed return, but they provide low interest rates. These low-interest but guaranteed investments should be just a small part (10 to 20 percent) of a conservative investment portfolio. After you have accumulated a serious amount of savings, you need to place these dollars in an investment such as a mutual fund with a great track record of growth.

8. Save 10 percent of your monthly income and place these funds in the highest interest savings plan available.

9. Begin to tithe 10 percent of your monthly income to your church in obedience to God's plan. Chapter 3 explains why tithing and charitable giving are the keys to achieving your goal of financial freedom.

10. Consider investing 20 percent of your investment funds in gold and silver coins as a conservative financial insurance policy. Another strategy is to choose a precious metals mutual fund. Remember, check Internet financial sites to find mutual funds that have demonstrated strong performance over the past five to ten years.

11. Complete up-to-date wills for you and your spouse drawn up by an experienced lawyer. Acquire adequate life and disability insurance to guarantee your income for your family. In addition, you should complete an enduring power of attorney as well as a power of attorney for personal care (for medical decisions). Chapters 10 and 11 discuss in greater detail the need for an up-to-date will and powers of attorney.

12. Research and acquire a high-quality long-term-care insurance policy that will provide for nursing home costs if necessary for you or your spouse in the future. This is one of the most important insurance needs

# BUSINESS REPLY MAIL
FIRST-CLASS MAIL PERMIT NO. 34   EDMOND OK

POSTAGE WILL BE PAID BY ADDRESSEE

**THE PHILADELPHIA TRUMPET**
**PO BOX 3700**
**EDMOND OK 73083-9943**

that must be addressed to protect your financial independence. Chapter 9 discusses in more depth the various types of insurance that you need.

Following a severe economic downturn, an investor with ample cash will be able to acquire excellent real estate and shares in solid companies at a fraction of the price they commanded before the upheaval. History reveals that those who survived the worst losses of the Great Depression were able to acquire valuable assets that became the foundation for significant wealth the rest of their lives.

## How Do Financially Successful People Really Live?

Most people imagine that those who are financially successful live a life of indulgent wealth, similar to Donald Trump or people featured on *Lifestyles of the Rich and Famous*. Movies and television shows project a vision of financial success that is based on pretense, illusion, credit, and the basic premise of "fake it till you make it!" In other words, present yourself as a financial success until you achieve the success. Too many people live on easily available credit while they anticipate achieving the financial results that will pay for their lavish lifestyle. Experience shows that this is a recipe for disaster.

Thomas J. Stanley in his book *The Millionaire Mind* reported on the actual lifestyles, decisions, habits, and character of Americans who achieved financial independence. Most people imagine that millionaires spend every dollar they earn and max out their lines of credit to support a lavish lifestyle. Stanley did find such a group of wealthy Americans who chose a credit-supported lifestyle far beyond their true economic resources. They borrowed money to finance a lifestyle based on their psychological need to impress themselves, their friends, and their neighbors. These people were characterized by high income, huge debt, and low net worth.

However, Stanley discovered that the vast majority of American millionaires lived quiet, conservative lives typified by high-quality houses, cars, and vacations that were far less costly than their millionaire status could have afforded. By maintaining a lifestyle below the level they could afford, they were able to build a solid financial base that would support their future life. These truly wealthy individuals are characterized by high income, little or no debt, and very high net worth.[4] Comparing the two groups, we see that excessive use of credit is the leading threat to financial independence.

Anyone living beyond his means needs to examine his financial status and be honest with himself about what he can afford. The inability to admit to others that you need to downsize your lifestyle to minimize debt and to gain control of your finances is one of the main impediments to making the vital changes that lead to financial freedom.

Goals are just wishes unless they are written down. When you write down your goals, it solidifies them and helps you commit seriously to accomplishing them. Use the statement of goals worksheet that follows to write out your financial and personal goals. Then commit your energies to achieving those goals.

Prime Minister Winston Churchill is famous for his bulldoglike tenacity of purpose that inspired England to stand firm against the Nazis during the darkest days of World War II. Churchill wrote, "Success is not final, failure is not fatal: it is the courage to continue that counts."[5]

## STATEMENT OF GOALS

**Date:** _____

### ONE-YEAR FINANCIAL GOALS

| | |
|---|---|
| Increase income to: | $_____ |
| Reduce total debt to: | $_____ |
| Build bank savings account to: | $_____ |
| Build investments to: | $_____ |
| Real estate total: | $_____ |
| Personal assets (household contents, boat, cars, etc.): | $_____ |
| | |
| Total assets: | $_____ |
| Total net worth in twelve months: | $_____ |

### FIVE-YEAR FINANCIAL GOALS

| | |
|---|---|
| Increase income to: | $_____ |
| Reduce total debt to: | $_____ |
| Build bank savings account to: | $_____ |
| Build investments to: | $_____ |
| Real estate total: | $_____ |
| Personal assets (household contents, boat, cars, etc.): | $_____ |
| | |
| Total assets: | $_____ |
| Total net worth in five years: | $_____ |

## ONE-YEAR PERSONAL GOALS

Physical (exercise, diet, weight reduction):

_____

Volunteer work:

_____

Vacation:

_____

Intellectual (reading, taking courses):

_____

Spiritual (Scripture study, prayer):

_____

Other:

_____


## FIVE-YEAR PERSONAL GOALS

Physical (exercise, diet, weight reduction):

_____

Volunteer work:

_____

Vacation:

_____

Intellectual (reading, taking courses):

_____

Spiritual (Scripture study, prayer):

_____

Other:

_____

## FINANCIAL BALANCE SHEET

To measure how well you are doing with your finances, you should calculate your net worth at least once a year. This will show you how much progress you are making toward your goal of financial independence.

Add up your total assets and deduct the amount of your total debts to arrive at your net worth. For example, if you have $220,000 in total assets, including the value of your home, car, furniture, and investments, and you owe a total of $120,000 on your mortgage, auto loan, credit cards, and other debts, then you have a net worth of $100,000. Improve your net worth by increasing your assets, reducing your debts, and implementing your financial goals and plans. You will find new motivation as you note your progress year after year.

**Date:** _____

### ASSETS

*Real Estate*

Principal residence:                                 $_____

Secondary residence (cottage, etc.):                 $_____

*Investments*

401(k):                                              $_____

IRA:                                                 $_____

Other (gold, silver, etc.):                          $_____

Equities or bonds:                                   $_____

Personal assets (household contents,
    boat, cars, etc.):                              $_____

Bank accounts:                                       $_____

Pension accounts:                                    $_____

Mutual funds:                                    $_____

Money-market funds:                              $_____

Certificates of deposit:                         $_____

Life insurance cash value:                       $_____

Other assets:                                    $_____

Total assets:                                    $_____

## LIABILITIES

Mortgages (principal and/or secondary):          $_____

Car or boat loans:                               $_____

Investment loans:                                $_____

Student loans, etc.:                             $_____

Personal loans:                                  $_____

Credit cards total:                              $_____

Total liabilities:                               $_____

## NET WORTH

Assets minus liabilities:                        $_____

# Chapter 3

# The Importance of Tithing and Charitable Giving

## *The Key to Financial Success*

*When it comes to giving,*
*some people will stop at nothing.*
—UNKNOWN

A recent study on giving habits found that only 4 percent of all church members tithe.[1] Not only does this lack of generosity rob Christians of the joy of giving; it also prevents them from experiencing God's promise of financial blessing.

For our parents' and grandparents' generations—who had far less financial prosperity—tithing was a deeply felt and loving obligation to God. In addition, they contributed funds to parachurch organizations, including missions and media broadcast ministries. During the last half of the last century, this mission effort resulted in the greatest explosion of world evangelism in the history of Christianity.

However, the baby-boom generation has not generally been taught the virtue of tithing. Thus most Christians in this generation have not learned the biblical necessity nor the spiritual benefits of giving 10 percent of their "increase" to God as their acknowledgment that they owe everything in their lives to God's provision and blessing. Along with the decline in teaching about the blessings of tithing, there has been a reduction in giving within the church and a drop in gifts to parachurch ministries. Therefore a huge number of vital evangelism ministries are suffering from lower financial support.

The principle of tithing is referred to forty times in the Word of God. Throughout the Bible, God promised blessings to the Jews when they obeyed His commands to offer the firstfruits of their harvest. God's Word records the Israelites' expectation of His blessings upon their lives due to their faithful response.

Tithing was actually practiced long before Moses revealed the Law to the Israelites at Mount Sinai. The Bible records that more than five hundred years earlier, the patriarch Abraham gave tithes to the priest-king Melchizedek as his gift to God. "And Melchizedek king of Salem brought forth bread and wine: and he was the priest of the most high God. And he blessed him, and said, Blessed be Abram of the most high God, possessor of heaven and earth: And blessed be the most high God, which hath delivered thine enemies into thy hand. And he gave him tithes of all" (Genesis 14:18–20).

## CHRISTIANS AND TITHING

Since the time of the sacrificial death of Jesus Christ on the Cross, Christians have been living under the principle of God's grace, not the Law of the Old Testament. However, the Bible clearly reveals that the character of God does not change. Therefore the principle that God blesses those who tithe remains unchanged. Our voluntary giving of our firstfruits and tithes to God acknowledges our willing allegiance to Him. And throughout the

Word of God, the Lord declares His commitment to bless those who acknowledge Him through their willing obedience to His commands: "Honour the LORD with thy substance, and with the firstfruits of all thine increase: So shall thy barns be filled with plenty, and thy presses shall burst out with new wine" (Proverbs 3:9–10). In the New Testament, the apostle Paul confirms that God's eternal principle of "sowing and reaping" applies to Christians even though we are no longer living under Law: "Be not deceived; God is not mocked: for whatsoever a man soweth, that shall he also reap. For he that soweth to his flesh shall of the flesh reap corruption; but he that soweth to the Spirit shall of the Spirit reap life everlasting. And let us not be weary in well doing: for in due season we shall reap, if we faint not" (Galatians 6:7–9).

Many wonder if Christians should still give a full 10 percent as a tithe. However, the Word of God clearly indicates that a tenth of our "increase" is the biblical tithe: "And all the tithe of the land, whether of the seed of the land, or of the fruit of the tree, is the LORD's: it is holy unto the LORD" (Leviticus 27:30). Indeed, the word *tithe* means "one tenth," not a portion or a piece, but a full 10 percent. While we are certainly no longer constrained by the Old Testament Law, God's principle of blessing our obedient giving remains as His unchangeable law.

Our gift of 10 percent demonstrates our awareness that the Lord actually owns 100 percent of what we have. In determining how much we should give back to the ministries of God, we should carefully consider how much God has given us. Everything we now have or ever will receive ultimately comes from the gracious provision of God. "For ye know the grace of our Lord Jesus Christ, that, though he was rich, yet for your sakes he became poor, that ye through his poverty might be rich" (2 Corinthians 8:9).

Many Christians ask, should we tithe based on our gross income or our net income after paying the taxes required by the government? Since Christians are not living spiritually under the Law, we should ask God for guidance as to what amount is appropriate. God promised that we would reap His blessings in direct proportion to the amount we sow. When I am asked this question in seminars, I often respond by asking, "Since the Lord has promised to bless us in response to His command that we tithe, the real question is this: do you want God to bless you in proportion to your net income or your gross?"

The tithe should be based on income not only from your paycheck but also from all your "increase," including investments and real-estate transactions. For example, if you sell your house for $300,000 at an increased value of $100,000 over your purchase price of $200,000, that is your "increase" (minus the costs you incurred). To follow biblical tithing principles, you should give God 10 percent of the increase: "Honour the LORD with thy substance, and with the firstfruits of all thine increase: So shall thy barns be filled with plenty" (Proverbs 3:9–10).

Remember that God accused Israel, His Chosen People, of robbing Him by refusing to pay the tithe through their gifts to the Temple. The prophet Malachi, quoting the words of God, warned the people of Israel:

> *Charity should begin at home, but should not stay there.*
> *—Philip Brooks*

"Will a man rob God? Yet ye have robbed me. But ye say, Wherein have we robbed thee? In tithes and offerings" (Malachi 3:8).

The Bible guides us first to pay our tithes and offerings to our local church, "the storehouse," where we are being spiritually fed and blessed. Then it's good to contribute to ministries or charities above the amount of our tithes. Before giving to a charity, however, always research its reputation for financial integrity and responsibility.

During my eighteen years as a professional financial planner, I had the privilege of interviewing several thousand businessmen and professionals about their financial affairs. Virtually all my clients who were Christians and who had achieved significant financial success acknowledged that one of the most important keys to achieving financial independence was giving 10 percent of their income to the Lord's ministries. It's also very interesting that some clients who acknowledged they tithed and who had achieved financial success were not even religious. They simply had learned that the universal principle of giving back 10 percent results in financial success. Tithing is the key to your success in achieving financial independence. Sadly, however, government statistics reveal that the average American household gives only 3 percent of its income to charity despite living in the wealthiest nation in history.[2]

The prophet Malachi gave this significant command of God in the closing book of the Old Testament: "Bring ye all the tithes into the storehouse, that there may be meat in mine house, and prove me now herewith, saith the LORD of hosts, if I will not open you the windows of heaven, and pour you out a blessing, that there shall not be room enough to receive it" (3:10). The Lord has committed Himself to prosper abundantly those who are faithful in their tithes to the House of God.

## CHRISTIANS AND CHARITY

Another foundational principle related to our prosperity is our willingness to give to others when they experience a financial crisis. The apostle John wrote, "But whoso hath this world's good, and seeth his brother have need, and shutteth up his bowels of compassion from him, how dwelleth the love of God in him? My little children, let us not love in word, neither in tongue; but in deed and in truth" (1 John 3:17–18).

Your attitude toward your money is a reflection of your attitude toward the Lord. The Christian who constantly blesses those around him will naturally find himself blessed by God. Too often we think of giving only in terms of placing our money in the offering plate at church or donating to a registered charitable fund that can issue a receipt to reduce our tax burden.

However, we need to be practical in our giving. The next time you see a Christian brother or sister in financial difficulties, prayerfully consider giving the person $100 (or whatever is appropriate) in addition to praying with him or her. Do not worry that you won't receive a charitable receipt to reduce your income taxes. The Lord keeps far better account of our giving than does the IRS. In the ancient book of Proverbs, God promises to bless those who demonstrate a generosity of spirit through their practical actions: "The liberal soul shall be made fat: and he that watereth shall be watered also himself" (11:25). The Lord will bless those who bless the work of God in organized ministries and in blessing people around them who are in need.

A story is told about a man who died and went to heaven. He was met at the Pearly Gates by Saint Peter, who led the man down the golden streets. They walked past mansion after beautiful mansion until they finally reached the end of the street, where they stopped in front of a modest wooden shack. The man asked Saint Peter why he got a shack when others were enjoying so many gold mansions. Saint Peter replied, "We did the best we could with the money you sent us."

# Chapter 4

# Setting Up Your Budget

*How Saving Builds Wealth Through Compound Interest*

*When your outgo exceeds your income,*
*then your upkeep will be your downfall.*
—BILL EARLE

It's a real struggle to gain control of your expenses relative to your income. But it's a necessary struggle, because you'll never achieve financial freedom unless you set up a budget that provides for regular savings. It is incredible to realize that 90 percent of American families live from paycheck to paycheck with almost no savings or investments. They are totally unprepared to deal with an emergency or the inevitable day when their salaried income will cease due to retirement, long-term disability, or premature death.

To gain control of your finances, establish a basic budget that will allow you to set targets, establish goals, and begin a savings program. Maintaining financial discipline will enable you to acquire enough savings to begin a practical investment plan. Many people have no idea where their money goes; their paycheck just seems to disappear every month. Someone once cynically said, "Living on a budget is exactly the same as living beyond your means, except now you will have a record of it." While budgeting does include keeping track of your spending, the benefit of a budget is that it enables you to control your spending and to purposely direct the financial resources God has provided.

I am not suggesting that you record every penny you spend. Rather, planning a family budget involves making basic decisions about allocating your monthly and annual income to various expected costs and then recording the end results. Author and speaker John Maxwell said this about the essence of budgeting: "A budget is people telling their money where to go instead of wondering where it went."[1] Bookstores, as well as many banks, have excellent budget books available to help you plan your monthly and yearly expenditures. The key to successful budgeting is to be flexible in your planning and to be realistic about the actual amounts you spend in various categories. Make sure you conservatively estimate your income but always overestimate your expenditures.

As you allot amounts for monthly expenditures, be certain also to budget for expenses that occur quarterly or annually. These include insurance-policy premiums, tax payments, college tuition, and other costs that occur other than monthly. A budget should not be a financial strait-jacket but a simple way to keep track of where your money is going so you can take control and redirect it in a way that helps achieve your goals. Preparing an annual budget with your spouse is an excellent way to discuss your goals and long-term plans as well as to reach a mutual understanding of your shared objectives.

The famous actor John Barrymore was provoked by financial difficulties arising from his uncertain and irregular income. He lamented, "Why is there so much month left at the end of the money?" The vast majority of American families spend far more every month than what they actually earn—about 10 percent more. This is a prescription for both family and national economic disaster.

If you want to break out of a debt-controlled life, you must control your spending. It is foolish to use consumer credit so you can spend more than your income. "There is treasure to be desired and oil in the dwelling of the wise; but a foolish man spendeth it up" (Proverbs 21:20). Debt results in bondage, and it's clear that financial bondage leads to spiritual bondage. "The rich ruleth over the poor, and the borrower is servant to the lender" (Proverbs 22:7). When you apply the principles in this book to get out of debt, you will experience a sense of freedom that is spiritually liberating.

Most families have so few financial reserves that a single emergency can quickly deplete their bank-account balances to zero. Therefore it is essential that you build up a reserve to ensure you have sufficient cash whenever a medical crisis or other emergency arises.

> *Money is better than poverty,*
> *if only for financial reasons.*
> *—Woody Allen*

A major key to beginning your plan for financial success is to discipline yourself to spend less than you earn. When you commit to doing this, the monthly surplus goes first into savings and ultimately into investments. A savings-and-investment program is essential to your financial independence.

## BEWARE OF THE $400,000 CAR!

Automobile costs can seriously damage your chances of achieving financial independence. If you choose to drive a used car, as many wise millionaires do, you will make significant progress toward financial success. One calculation suggests that you could end up with as much as $400,000 in additional retirement funds at age sixty-five by investing the difference between what you would pay annually for a brand-new car every three years and what you would pay for a similar reliable car that you replace once every ten years.

## The Power and Peril of Compound Interest

Understanding the power of compound interest is fundamental to a successful investment strategy. Significantly, Baron Rothschild, one of the richest men in history, described compound interest as the "eighth wonder of the world." If you allow yourself to become mired in growing debt, compound interest will work against you. But if you use it to your advantage, compound interest is a powerful financial principle that will multiply the savings-and-investment funds you set aside every month.

For example, if you could save and invest $1,000 every year (only $83.33 per month) from age thirty-five to age sixty-five at an average return of 10 percent, you would accumulate $164,494 by the time you retire. A similar investment of $5,000 every year at 10 percent from age thirty-five to age sixty-five would accumulate $822,470. To earn this rate of return, remember that your bank savings account should be only a temporary place to store your funds while you accumulate an amount to invest. Once your bank account has grown to a balance between $2,500 and $5,000, you should explore investment options that will provide much higher interest or investment returns. Many of these investment options will be explored in chapter 7.

# Chapter 5

# The Use and Abuse of Credit

*You Can Get Out of Debt Forever*

*The borrower is servant to the lender.*
—PROVERBS 22:7

In many religious circles, the use of credit has been unfairly demonized. While credit can be abused, it is unwise to overlook its usefulness in furthering your life goals when it is used properly. The prudent use of credit is essential to your quality of life, since it allows you to purchase a large asset, such as a home or a car. However, the unwise and casual use of credit encourages people to purchase depreciating consumer items—such as televisions, electronic devices, and furniture—that they would be wise to delay buying until they have the ability to acquire these items with cash.

Unfortunately, the misuse of credit (especially easily acquired credit cards) has brought many couples to the brink of financial disaster. Marriage counselors tell us that arguments over money, increasing debts, and excessive credit-card bills are major areas of conflict in marriage, often leading to divorce. Because family finances are integral to every other area of life, controlling the use of credit and creating financial stability with wise investments can enormously improve your marriage, your family relationships, and your spiritual life as you invest in your family's needs.

The Bible warns against excessive debt because of the financial and spiritual bondage it creates. God commands us to pay our bills when they are due. Further, we should not delay our repayment of debt if we have the ability to repay. The Scriptures declare, "Withhold not good from them to whom it is due, when it is in the power of thine hand to do it. Say not unto thy neighbour, Go, and come again, and to morrow I will give; when thou hast it by thee" (Proverbs 3:27–28). If you are honestly unable to pay a debt on time, call your lender to explain. Then confirm in writing that you have a legitimate problem and indicate clearly when you will make the required payment.

Creditors will usually cooperate with you if you are facing a genuine, temporary financial problem. However, lenders become annoyed when a person falls behind in monthly payments and does not explain the reason for the delay. The common habit of most debtors who fall behind is silence and avoidance rather than communicating with their creditors. This is actually the worst thing you can do. The payment of even a small part of the outstanding loan assures your creditor that you acknowledge your debt and are committed to paying it. Your reputation for paying your bills on time is vital to a strong credit rating, which is an important tool in building your financial independence. Reliability in paying your bills is also critical to your reputation and the effectiveness of your Christian testimony.

## OBTAINING CREDIT FOR THE FIRST TIME OR
## AFTER YOU'VE HAD CREDIT PROBLEMS

If you are attempting to obtain credit for the first time—or following past credit problems (including bankruptcy)—prepare carefully before approaching a credit institution.

1. Prepare a financial summary that includes all your listed assets, both monetary—bank accounts, 401(k)s, etc.—and any real property. Also list all outstanding liabilities. Calculate your resulting net worth as discussed in chapter 2.

2. List all of your monthly expenses from your budget. Make certain you have enough excess income to easily support the payments that would arise from any new loan.

3. Also include your total monthly income from all sources, together with the length of your employment in a company as well as in that industry. Document your income with a copy of your last income-tax return and written income verification from your employer. If your employment is fairly recent, a letter confirming your employment will assist you in the credit evaluation process.

4. Include the length of time you have lived at your present address. The longer, the better.

5. Prior to applying for new credit, always request your latest credit-bureau report from all three major credit-reporting agencies. This allows you to review these reports for errors and to arrange to correct any inaccurate or outdated information. If there is negative information in your credit report, discuss with the bureau representatives exactly what documentation you need to provide in order to dispute and correct any incorrect information. You may need to contact a past creditor to obtain a letter confirming that a past credit problem has been solved. Attach any such correction letter to your credit-preparation file, and bring all this data to your interview with the potential creditor.

Be prepared to present to the credit bureau written receipts that demonstrate all disputed bills with past creditors have been paid. You can also request a form from the credit bureau to ask them to verify directly with the past creditor that the disputed bill was paid. If you cannot get a creditor to verify to the credit bureau that your problem has been resolved, then your only option is to prepare a short statement explaining the reason for the disputed matter (such as an extended illness, death in the family, or temporary inability to work) and submit the statement to the credit bureau to add to your file. When a potential creditor makes an inquiry in the future, your explanation will be seen along with the rest of the file.

You may request a free credit report once a year from all three major credit-reporting agencies.

- Equifax Credit Information Services Inc., P.O. Box 740241, Atlanta, GA 30374-0241, 800-685-1111, www.equifax.com
- Experian, 888-397-3742, www.experian.com
- TransUnion Corporation Consumer Disclosure Center, P.O. Box 2000, Chester, PA 19022, 800-888-4213; www.transunion.com[1]

6. Be certain to pay any past-due income taxes before applying for new credit. Potential lenders are usually reluctant to lend money to anyone who owes back taxes.

By going to the credit interview prepared with these items, you will demonstrate to the lender that you are a serious applicant. This will make it much easier for the lender to quickly grant you credit that is appropriate to your risk profile.

In establishing your credit the first time or after past credit problems, it is often easier to acquire a low-limit credit card from a department store or oil company than from one of the major credit-card companies. These cards usually offer a lower credit limit ($500 or less) than the major credit-card companies do (usually $1,000 or more). Once you have demonstrated your credit worthiness by using the department-store or oil-company credit card (even though it typically comes with a higher interest rate) and promptly paying your charges for up to a year, you will be in a much better position to successfully apply for a major credit card.

Many people believe that receiving preapproved credit-card offers are a plus in building their credit worthiness. Unfortunately, the more credit cards you acquire, the less new credit is actually available to you. Even if you totally pay off your credit cards each month, your possession of multiple credit cards creates the possibility in the minds of potential creditors that you might choose to maximize all available credit from every card at some point. This causes credit-granting companies to add up the credit potential of all your cards (even if you are not using them) and consider this credit potential in their evaluation of a new loan. If you don't need a particular credit card, it would be wise to cancel that card.

## Credit-Reporting Agencies and Credit Scores

In addition to checking your current credit report, virtually all lenders will also obtain a credit score on you as a prospective borrower. The score is determined by a mathematical equation that evaluates the available information in your credit report. Lenders compare your personal credit information with that of tens of thousands of other credit reports on file and obtain a credit score that predicts mathematically the likelihood of your paying back the loan in a timely manner. Your credit score attempts to identify your level of future credit risk.

The three major credit-reporting agencies (Equifax, Experian, and TransUnion) call these credit scores FICO scores because the numbers are generated by computer software that was created by Fair Isaac Corporation. A credit-score calculation requires up-to-date (last six months) information on your current payment patterns.

Lenders believe that FICO scores provide them with the best predictor of your future risk of nonpayment. The higher your FICO score, the lower the risk to the lender, and the greater the likelihood that you will get the loan and be able to negotiate a lower interest rate. Since every lender has its own policy regarding credit evaluation, you cannot be certain how the lender will evaluate a particular FICO score.

The three major credit bureaus describe their credit scoring using different names, but they are always ultimately based on the Fair Isaac Corporation scoring model.

| CREDIT-REPORTING AGENCY | FICO SCORE |
|---|---|
| Equifax | BEACON |
| Experian | Experian/Fair Isaac Risk Model |
| TransUnion | EMPIRICA |

Your current credit scores can vary among the three major agencies because the information each agency has on you will differ. As the credit bureau learns new information about your credit, it will alter your FICO score. If you are planning a major purchase (a house, for example), you would be wise to check with the various credit bureaus to learn what your current FICO score is before applying to a lender.

The Federal Trade Commission recommends that you check your personal credit report and your FICO score with the three credit bureaus at least twice a year. Up to 70 percent of credit reports (and thus your FICO scores) contain errors. When you protect your credit by eliminating errors, you will be able to save significant amounts on loans and insurance premiums. You can check your current credit report and FICO score by contacting the credit bureaus listed earlier in this chapter or by accessing this Web site: www.freecreditreports.com.

You have the legal right to review your own credit report whenever you want. You should automatically request your up-to-date report in writing and bring it with you (after any needed corrections have been made) to your credit interview with your bank or mortgage broker. You can request your updated credit report from each of the credit bureaus as often as needed without adversely affecting your credit profile.

An improved credit score and clean credit report can save a considerable amount in interest rates on your mortgage. For example, if you have a thirty-year fixed-rate mortgage for $300,000, your improved FICO score will result in major savings:

| YOUR FICO SCORE | MONTHLY PAYMENT | INTEREST RATE |
| --- | --- | --- |
| 720+ | $1,733 | 5.66% |
| 675 | $1,861 | 6.32% |
| 650 | $2,091 | 7.47% |
| Less than 620 | $2,313 | 8.53% |

By obtaining a FICO score of 720 or higher, you would save up to $580 every month compared to a person who has a FICO score of less than 620.[2] Over the course of a thirty-year mortgage, this higher FICO score would save you an impressive $208,080 in interest payments.

When you get into trouble with a creditor due to late payments or missed payments, this negative information is automatically recorded at these credit-reporting agencies. This information remains current in your file for seven years. However, declaring personal bankruptcy stays on your credit record for ten years. When a credit-granting company requests your report from the three credit-reporting agencies (with your written permission), the request is indicated at the end of the credit report. Credit insiders call this a "hit." If you apply for a loan with a significant number of banks within a few months, the evidence of these hits will alert subsequent lending institutions that you are probably an active "credit seeker," as they define it. That is a negative factor when a bank or mortgage company evaluates your credit risk.

You can improve your FICO score by doing the following:

- Always pay your bills on time.
- Check with all three credit bureaus annually to be certain that any inaccurate information is found and corrected.
- Make certain that your credit-card balances are kept as low as possible.
- Avoid applying for a number of loans or credit cards at the same time.
- Have at least one credit card or loan that demonstrates a good track record of timely payments.
- Avoid applying for credit cards if you don't really need them.

### Your Debt-to-Income Ratio (DTI)

Banks and other credit-issuing companies use a number of ratios and formulas to determine your credit worthiness. One of the ratios is the debt-to-income (DTI) ratio, which helps determine your credit profile. Banks use this ratio to calculate how much more debt you can safely afford. The DTI ratio is the amount of household debt (excluding your mortgage) compared to your household income. If 30 percent of your pretax gross monthly household income goes each month toward paying debt, then your debt-to-income ratio is 30 percent. A low DTI ratio indicates financial strength.

> *If money be not thy servant, it will be thy master. The covetous man cannot so properly be said to possess wealth, as that may be said to possess him.*
> —*Francis Bacon*

An excellent DTI ratio is generally below 20 percent. If you're paying 20–25 percent of your total joint income to service debt, the banks are going to look with favor on your credit application. In most cases you will be able to negotiate lower interest rates and better loan terms. However, if the credit agencies calculate that your DTI ratio is higher than 30 percent, your ability to borrow might be jeopardized for a major purchase like a house. When your DTI ratio is greater than 36 percent, it will be virtually impossible to borrow funds from most banks. If your DTI ratio is higher than 50 percent, avoid applying for any additional credit. Virtually all creditors will reject a loan request from anyone with a DTI that exceeds 50 percent.

## A Practical Plan to Gain Control of Your Credit

The following steps will go a long way toward keeping your credit under control and moving you toward long-term financial independence.

1. Before making a major consumer purchase, always ask yourself: Do I really need to buy this item right now with expensive credit? Can I wait and purchase this item later with cash? If you are about to buy a depreciating item with credit, first calculate very conservatively how much of your monthly income you can safely devote to credit-interest payments. In making this calculation, allow a safety margin of more than 10 percent of your monthly income to be placed in reserve in your bank savings account above your normal expenses, tithing, and existing credit obligations.

2. Shop very carefully for loans and credit cards since interest rates, user fees, and credit terms vary widely. Check the total cost of your current credit cards against the cost of cards offered by other lenders. Shop as carefully for your credit as you would shop for the best deal on a car. Some credit cards charge 24 percent or higher in interest charges (despite the fact that major banks can obtain funds at a cost of less than 2 percent).

Additionally, when you have a checking account with a bank, avoid using the overdraft privileges. The interest rate charged for overdrafts is often extremely high.

3. Avoid the credit-card trap that encourages tens of millions of consumers to habitually carry large credit-card balances from month to month. The extremely costly habit of paying only the minimum required monthly

payment leads to financial bondage. Smart users pay off the full balance of their credit cards every month. They are obtaining free of charge a full record of their purchases, courtesy of the credit-card company. Plus the cardholder has use of the bank's funds interest free for possibly thirty days, sometimes longer.

Ideally you should use no more than two major credit cards, including one of the universally accepted cards such as Visa, MasterCard, Discover Card, or American Express. If your credit-card balances have grown so high that you cannot pay them down to zero in a few months, consider arranging a personal bank loan or a personal line of credit at a much lower interest rate. Use those funds to pay off the outstanding balances on your credit cards. Then repay the new low-interest bank loan as quickly as possible. However, do not allow a zero balance on your credit card to tempt you to make unwise purchases. Make sure you keep your credit-card balances at a level that you can pay off in full each month.

4. Avoid using credit for consumer items that depreciate quickly, such as a television, furniture, or appliances. You should simply wait until you can buy the item with cash. Paying with cash reinforces your appreciation of the actual cost of the purchase and leads you to be prudent in future purchases.

5. Use credit wisely, primarily to acquire major items such as a home or car that you could not practically purchase otherwise.

6. Whenever you choose to borrow, make certain that you arrange to pay off the loan as quickly as you can to minimize the total cost of borrowing. The disciplined homeowner who arranges to make significant prepayments on his mortgage can save an enormous amount of future interest charges and pay off his mortgage many years earlier. This issue is covered in greater detail in chapter 6.

Credit is a lot like fire. When you are in control of it, credit can be an extremely valuable servant. However, when credit is out of control, it can ruin your life. "According to the Federal Reserve, by 1999, more than 42 percent of the baby boomers averaged $11,616 in credit card debt."[3]

## THE TRUE COSTS OF CREDIT-CARD INTEREST

Recent studies indicate that the average American uses up to nine credit cards. Up to two hundred million credit cards are used every day, mostly to acquire nonessential consumer items. Studies also indicate that 55 to 75 percent of Americans carry unpaid balances on their credit cards every month, which means they are paying an astounding amount of interest every year.

Other studies suggest that the average household is carrying more than $8,000 of credit-card debt and is paying more than 15 percent average interest on this debt.[4] Up to $1 million is now being charged on credit cards by American consumers every *minute*. This adds up to a staggering $480 billion of credit-card debt every year, while the U.S. savings rate has dropped to almost zero. According to an article in the *Charlotte Observer*, the average American family saves only .2 percent of its disposable income—only $1.80 per week for a family with $50,000 in take-home pay.[5]

Some studies suggest that the use of credit cards to purchase consumer items results in an increase of up to 30 percent in the cost of the particular consumer item by the time the purchase is fully paid for, including both the initial price and accumulated interest charges. An Internet site that examines the cost of credit provides a remarkable example: "A $2,000 sofa financed at 19.8 percent interest with minimum monthly payments will take 31 years and 2 months to pay off and you will pay more than $10,000. The interest alone robs you of $8,202 that you sweat for decades to earn. In fact, you will have to earn about $12,000 gross to net $8,202 for the interest just so you can have your $2,000 sofa. What could possibly be worth paying 5 times its value?"[6]

## Warnings About Debit Cards

Many people use debit cards instead of paying with cash or writing checks. If you use a debit card, keep in mind that the funds will be deducted instantly from your bank account. Also, when you use a debit card at a store, make certain that the store will not charge you an extra fee. And be aware that many stores outside of North America will not accept debit cards.

Most issuers of debit cards charge fees for transactions that are comparable to those charged for automated-teller transactions. However, some debit cards issued to valued bank customers instead carry a flat annual fee of approximately $25.

## Pitfalls to Avoid When Getting Out of Debt

As you stick to a budget and control your spending with the goal of eliminating debt, be careful that you don't walk into any of the following traps.

### Debt-Consolidation Plans

For most people, debt consolidation is useless. It's usually a case of treating the obvious symptom while leaving the underlying cause untreated. Taking out a large loan to consolidate and repay numerous small loans and credit-card balances often encourages borrowers to continue to build up new credit-card balances, since new credit is freed up after they pay off the original outstanding balances. Some experts estimate that more than 75 percent of people reaccumulate their credit-card debt after they have acquired a debt-consolidation loan.

The first step you must take to solve a lifestyle problem is to honestly face the fact that you have a problem. Then resolve to change the financial habits that have produced this problem. The basic cause of out-of-control debt is the bad habit of spending more than you earn by using credit and failing to develop a committed savings-and-investment program.

### Debt-Management Companies and Credit-Repair Schemes

Television, Internet, and print ads offer to manage your out-of-control debt and repair the damage to your credit rating caused by your past poor credit habits. These schemes cannot really repair your credit situation, since the credit-reporting agencies will correct only the actual errors in your credit record. Since it was your poor financial habits that got you into trouble, help will come only when you commit to new habits to live within your means and avoid credit except for the purchase of a car or house.

Debt-management companies propose to accept one monthly payment from you, saying they will negotiate with each of your creditors to arrange better interest rates and lower monthly payments. While this can sometimes stop the harassment from creditors, it will destroy your credit history. Future creditors assume that your using a debt-management company indicates that you have refused to deal with your past debt responsibilities. Most mortgage lenders, for example, regard the involvement of a debt-management company with your credit account on the same scale as if you had declared bankruptcy. In addition, the Better Business Bureaus have numerous consumer complaints on file against such companies.

### Verbal Promises of Collection Agencies

When people get into serious trouble with their credit, they are often confronted by credit-collection agencies. For those who face this unpleasant experience, a word to the wise is in order. Do not trust the spoken promises of any collection agency employee. Always demand that any promises be received in writing before you act on their promise of what will occur when you make the agreed payment on outstanding debt. The history of those who have relied on oral agreements with collection agency employees indicates that their spoken promises have no legal authority and little likelihood of being honored.

## BANKRUPTCY: WHEN IS IT AN OPTION?

In the case of a person who suffers a disability that forces him to cease his business activities, or pursuant to a catastrophic business failure where the owner has personally guaranteed the company's loans, an individual may be forced to declare bankruptcy. However, most people declare personal bankruptcy to escape the consumer debts they have unwisely accumulated.

It is appalling that millions of people have declared bankruptcy to escape relatively small debt amounts. *Money Magazine* reported that "90% of all personal bankruptcies could have been avoided with just an extra $250 in monthly income."[7] Every year produces another record number of personal bankruptcy filings. In 2002, bankruptcies outpaced the previous year's amount of 1,398,864 by 7.8 percent, or 1,508,578.

When someone declares Chapter 7 bankruptcy (complete bankruptcy with no plan to recover or repay creditors), their default on their creditors remains on their credit report for ten years, which normally makes it impossible for them to obtain credit. Such a bankruptcy declaration produces serious problems far beyond the ten-year mark. Many job application forms and most credit applications ask if you have *ever* declared bankruptcy, and this fact will seriously damage your credit record and employment opportunities for decades.

A person *must* declare if he or she had a personal bankruptcy when asked on a credit or legal questionnaire. The failure to answer this question honestly subjects the applicant to the charge of financial fraud. Therefore do everything you can to avoid bankruptcy. Instead of pursuing bankruptcy, do your best to negotiate with creditors to repay your loans over time. Many creditors will accept partial payment to settle an outstanding file rather than face the prospect of receiving no payment at all.

Tragically, the most common cause of bankruptcy for most Americans is a personal disability resulting from an injury or illness. Prior to age sixty-five, it is far more likely that you will suffer a serious disability than premature death. If you are in your thirties, you are twelve times more likely to suffer a disruption in your income from disability than from early death.

## YOUR CHANCES OF SUFFERING A DISABILITY

The odds of experiencing at least one long-term disability (three months or longer) before you reach the age of sixty-five are as follows:

| Age | Probability |
| --- | --- |
| 25 | 44% |
| 30 | 42% |
| 35 | 41% |
| 40 | 39% |
| 45 | 36% |
| 50 | 33% |
| 55 | 27%[8] |

Yet most Americans never seriously consider the risk to their income or their family's financial future that arises from a physical disability. As we will examine in chapter 9, the risk to your financial plans is so great that you need to plan to protect yourself and your family through disability insurance. This insurance will provide a guaranteed income in the event that accident or disease prevents your continued employment.

## Getting Out of Debt Forever

The power of inertia in human behavior is hard to exaggerate. Most people are so reluctant to change their behavior that they will remain mired in a hopeless financial disaster rather than commit themselves to radically changing their spending and savings habits. If you continue the same financial habits that brought you into deep debt, then your life will remain a financial disaster zone. Your financial situation today is the direct result of the decisions and actions you made over the past few years. The only way to seriously improve your financial lifestyle is to radically change your old habits into new, positive money habits that will lead you toward your goal of financial independence.

### Attitudes Toward Debt

While it is natural human behavior "to want it now," financial maturity requires us to recognize that many of our desired purchases should wait until we can afford to pay for them with cash. Unfortunately, advertising and marketing encourage us to purchase on credit whatever we desire, even though we don't have the money to pay for it.

The easy-credit industry captures hundreds of millions of consumers through a natural, but sinful, desire known as greed. In this regard, we're not unlike the lower primates. Natives of South Pacific islands have an ingenious method for capturing monkeys. An islander empties the milk from a coconut by cutting a small hole in the side of the fruit. He then places inside several nuts that monkeys love to eat. After reattaching the coconut to a tree with a small wire, the native waits for a monkey to approach. The monkey places his paw through the hole to grasp the bait. With his now-clenched fist, he cannot extract his paw from the coconut.

Although the monkey has to do nothing more than release the nuts to free himself from the trap, he remains there until he is captured. Greed captures the monkey just as it captures millions of Americans in a lifetime of slavery to debt as a consequence of the unwise use of credit.

A fascinating survey of the Forbes 400 reported the attitudes toward debt and credit that were held by the four hundred wealthiest people in the United States. Despite the widespread myth that the use of debt is a key to financial progress, 75 percent of the wealthiest Americans believed that the best method of building wealth and financial success was to avoid debt and remain debt free.[9]

Among the thousands of financially successful people I interviewed, I cannot recall any who indicated that they used personal debt in any significant way to achieve their financial independence. That does not mean they never used credit. However, debt was never a significant part of their strategy to achieve financial independence. The interviews revealed that these successful people had learned to live within their current income and avoid consumer debt. They used credit for their mortgage and occasionally for their car, but they paid for consumer purchases in cash.

The first step on your road to financial independence is to honestly acknowledge that your biggest problem is your accumulated debt for credit cards, car loans, mortgages, and so forth. The second step is to acknowledge the danger of obtaining additional debt. There is little point in sacrificing to pay off existing debts if you replace those debts with newly acquired loans. If you want to achieve financial independence, you need to destroy the "living in debt" habits that have imprisoned so many in our society.

The clients I counseled often indicated that they could not save because there was so little money left after they paid their living costs and debt payments. I would ask them to add up the amounts they were paying monthly for each credit card, car loan, and mortgage. Then, when I asked if they could save and invest if they could free up that amount of money, the solution became obvious.

We must refuse to buy things on credit and learn to purchase possessions only when we have the money in our accounts. This is one reason to use a debit card rather than a credit card. Using a debit card gives you the convenience of a credit card without tempting you to increase your debt. A debit card reminds you that each purchase adds immediately to your expenses as well as bank service charges.

### Steps to Freedom

To begin the process of getting out of debt forever, seriously cut down on the precious dollars that are being spent on credit payments. To limit the amount you devote to servicing debt, list all your debts using the form at the end of this chapter. In the second column, list the name of each creditor, the remaining principal amount owed on that debt, and the rate of interest you are paying. Your credit-card statements and loan statements will identify the annual rate of interest.

Now rework your list by starting at the top of the page with the debt that has the smallest amount outstanding. Then list your other debts in ascending order, based on the amount still owed on each one. Dave Ramsey, a well-respected financial writer, explains the principle of paying off your debts one at a time, beginning with the smallest—even if it has the lowest rate of interest. While he acknowledges the advantage of wiping out the loans with the highest interest rates first, he believes (and he may be right) that the motivational value to continue this debt-reduction program is much greater when you eliminate the smallest debt first. Then use the freed-up monthly funds to attack the next smallest debt on your list.[10]

An alternative, if you're highly disciplined, is to attack the debt with the highest interest rate first. Though it may take longer to pay that one off, it will save you many dollars in interest costs. No matter how you eliminate your debts, getting one loan or credit-card balance out of the way will motivate you to continue on with the next one, eliminating your oppressive debt burden much more quickly than if you continue to live in financial bondage.

## USE CREDIT TO YOUR ADVANTAGE

The advantage of having a major credit card is that it is accepted virtually everywhere. In addition, major credit cards provide their clients powerful protection against fraud. For example, Visa adopted a zero-liability policy in 2000 that protects its clients against fraudulent activity on their credit and debit cards. If someone misuses the cardholder's account, the cardholder is protected against financial liability, even if the client fails to immediately notify the company of the fraudulent activity.

For many people, however, a debit card is preferable to a credit card. While you might need a credit card to rent a car, many of the smaller car-rental firms will accept a debit card. Likewise, you can usually purchase items on the Internet or pay for a hotel room with a debit card. It is always wise to inquire in advance about the company's policy on accepting debit cards.

Debit cards are extremely helpful to those who have had trouble controlling their use of credit. Limiting yourself to a debit card forces you to avoid purchasing items unless you already have the cash in your bank account.

Remember, the hardest but most significant step on your road to financial freedom is taking control of your debt. Paying off your credit cards and other nonmortgage debt will free you to use those funds to systematically invest in a great mutual fund or other investment vehicle.

## STATEMENT OF DEBTS

Date:_____

| LIABILITY | NAME OF CREDITOR | OUTSTANDING BALANCE | INTEREST RATE |
|---|---|---|---|
| Home Mortgage | | | |
| Secondary Mortgage | | | |
| Automobile Loan | | | |
| Boat or Consumer Loan | | | |
| Other Loan | | | |
| Other Loan | | | |
| Visa | | | |
| MasterCard | | | |
| American Express | | | |
| Other Debt | | | |
| Other Debt | | | |
| Other Debt | | | |
| **Total Debt** | | | |

## *Two Debt-Reduction Strategies*

Rearrange the list of liabilities from top to bottom with the highest interest rate at the top and the lowest interest rate at the bottom. One debt-reduction approach is to begin by applying all available funds each month to aggressively pay down the debt with the highest interest rate. Then, after eliminating that debt, use all available monthly funds to pay down the loan with the next-highest interest rate. Continue until each debt is paid off.

A second strategy is to begin by applying all available funds each month to aggressively pay off the debt with the lowest outstanding balance. Then use the freed funds to attack the next-smallest debt and so on. The idea is that by aggressively eliminating your debts one by one, you will gain motivation to continue paying off the larger debts.

## Strategy No. 1

Date:_____

| Liabilities Listed by Interest Rates | Name of Creditor | Outstanding Balance | Interest Rate |
|---|---|---|---|
| Highest Interest Rate | | | |
| Next-Highest Interest Rate | | | |
| Third-Highest Interest Rate *(continue in descending order of interest rate)* | | | |
| Other Loan | | | |
| Other Loan | | | |
| Other Loan | | | |
| Other Loan | | | |
| Other Loan | | | |
| Other Debt | | | |
| Other Debt | | | |
| Other Debt | | | |
| **Total Debt** | | | |

## STRATEGY No. 2

Date:_____

| LIABILITIES LISTED BY OUTSTANDING BALANCE | NAME OF CREDITOR | OUTSTANDING BALANCE | INTEREST RATE |
|---|---|---|---|
| Lowest Balance | | | |
| Next-Highest Balance | | | |
| Next-Highest Balance *(continue in ascending order of outstanding balance)* | | | |
| Other Loan | | | |
| Other Loan | | | |
| Other Loan | | | |
| Other Loan | | | |
| Other Loan | | | |
| Other Debt | | | |
| Other Debt | | | |
| Other Debt | | | |
| **Total Debt** | | | |

# Chapter 6

---

# Getting Smart About Homeownership and Mortgages

*How to Make Your Home Your Best Investment*

*If you think no one cares you're alive,*
*try missing a couple of house payments.*
—UNKNOWN

For most people, a home mortgage is the largest single investment they will ever make. And we all know that owning a home is one of life's fondest dreams. Since this dream comes with such a high price tag, it is vital that those who seek financial freedom carefully examine their options in repaying their mortgage so they can arrive as quickly as possible at the point where they own their home free and clear.

Kaye and I remember the moment we repaid our mortgage as one of the most significant steps on our journey toward true financial independence. The tremendous experience of knowing that we no longer owed a monthly mortgage payment but rather totally owned our home was a memorable milestone.

Homeownership is one of the best financial investments available to the average investor. One of the keys to success in real estate is to lock in your profits at the time you purchase the property. If you buy the right property at the right time at the right price, you will virtually be guaranteed a profitable investment.

Research is the key. Find the best real-estate agent in your community and cultivate a good relationship with him or her. Buy quality real estate from a motivated seller—someone who has a legitimate motive to sell that particular property quickly. Discover through friendly questions the seller's real motivation to sell. You can often determine the seller's real motivation by listening carefully. Look for revealing details, such as a job transfer to another state, the couple's last child leaving the nest, a divorce, or the loss of a job. Such changes in life circumstances usually signal the need for the homeowner to sell the property quickly.

There is a useful question that can reveal a seller's true motivation. After listening to the seller's first answer to why he wants to sell, ask, "In addition to that, is there any other reason you wish to sell your home at this time?" Once you understand the seller's real motive, you can move toward a win-win arrangement. He can obtain what he wants while you obtain what you want.

## How Much Can You Afford to Spend for a House?

In deciding how much of a home you can afford, consider this rule of thumb: your down payment should be approximately 25 percent of the total price of the house. If you can afford it, an excellent choice is to invest more than 25 percent of the purchase price. Mortgage lenders usually calculate your ability to afford a given mortgage payment by applying a formula they call the gross debt service ratio. The basic rule is that you can afford to spend a maximum of 30 percent of your gross monthly income on your combined mortgage payment, including real-estate taxes. Many mortgage lenders require the buyer to escrow both the real-estate taxes and the homeowner's insurance on a prorated basis with every monthly payment. Some lenders even require that the borrower take out a decreasing term life insurance policy in the amount of the sum borrowed. The cost of the life insurance policy is then added to the monthly amount the buyer has to send to the mortgage company.

An additional measure of your ability to comfortably handle your mortgage payments is known as the total debt service ratio formula. This formula says that your total payments for indebtedness—including other loans, credit cards, and mortgage payment plus real-estate taxes—should not exceed 40 percent of your gross monthly income. The ratios that mortgage lenders use to qualify home buyers also serve as an excellent guideline for you to determine how much you can afford to spend on a home.

A useful rule of thumb is that you should not spend more than three times your annual salary on the purchase price of a home. When you apply for a mortgage, you also need to keep in mind that your mortgage payments are only part of the annual cost of owning a home. Other expenses include the one-time cost of title insurance, which most mortgage lenders will require you to pay; the ongoing cost of homeowner's insurance; utilities, including water, electricity, gas, and garbage pickup; the various needed repairs to your home that include everything from roof, plumbing, electrical, heating, and possibly landscaping; and in some neighborhoods, dues to a homeowners' association. If you have previously lived in rental housing, you may easily underestimate these new hidden costs that will become your responsibility.

## How to Make Your Mortgage Work for You

Homeownership is one of the most powerful tools for achieving financial independence. Most of us could never purchase a house unless we borrowed the funds. Unfortunately, the normal mortgage amortization schedule establishes a pattern of mortgage payments over the next twenty-five to thirty years. This results in the average homeowner paying interest equal to two or three times the original cost of the home! During the first few years following your purchase of a home, virtually all of your monthly payments go toward the interest with almost no significant reduction of the outstanding mortgage balance.

For example, with a typical term of twenty-five years on a $100,000 mortgage bearing a fixed interest rate of 8.5 percent, the homeowner will make payments of $805 every month for twenty-five years, totaling an amazing $241,568.13 before he owns his home free and clear. He will pay for his home two and a half times! Ask your mortgage lender to provide you with a full amortization schedule showing the actual amount from each mortgage payment that goes toward repaying the principal. Looking at the amortization schedule should motivate you to prepay your mortgage as quickly as possible.

The word *mortgage* is derived from two Latin words: *mortuus*, which relates to "death," and *gage*, which means "attachment" or "pledge." In other words, *mortgage* refers to the grip that is financially associated with property and death. Anyone with a mortgage would be wise to pay off the outstanding balance as quickly as possible.

> *I've got all the money I'll ever need, if I die by four o'clock.*

Making voluntary prepayments on your mortgage is one of the most significant and effective investment decisions you can make. Your savings on future interest charges will be astronomical. In effect, you are depositing your prepayments into your own private bank by increasing your equity investment in your home. If you should ever need to access emergency funds, you can borrow against your increased home equity. The key to saving significant amounts of interest on your mortgage is to reduce the amortization period by voluntarily increasing your mortgage payments. Surprisingly, only 3 percent of homeowners choose to save interest by pre-paying their mortgage.

Consider the situation of a typical homeowner. Bob has a twenty-five-year $100,000 mortgage at 9 percent interest. By making a prepayment of only $1,200 every year, Bob will save $50,365 in interest and pay off his mortgage in only eighteen years. Since most other available investments will usually be taxable, assuming a tax rate of 40 percent, Bob would have to earn 15 percent before tax on a taxable investment of $1,200 to achieve the same economic benefit as prepaying $1,200 annually on his mortgage. Very few investments will provide the same security and flexibility and guarantee such a high rate of return as prepaying your mortgage.

## Strategies to Enhance Your Investment in Your Home

It's astounding how much mortgage interest costs increase the amount you pay for your home. According to the Web site www.about.com:

A 30 year mortgage for a $175,000 home at 8% has a monthly payment of about $1,500.00. With 25 years to go, the monthly interest on this loan is about $1,390. That means that the friendly loan officer will be charging $1,390 for the use of their $110 this month. What a deal! If you think I'm kidding, look at your payment or ask the bank how much is going to interest and how much to principal; or check out the following examples.

- 30 year 8% mortgage after 15 years, the monthly interest [portion] is 77%
- 25 year 7% mortgage after 5 years, the monthly interest [portion] is 91%

- 20 year 10% mortgage after 10 years, the monthly interest [portion] is 73%
- 30 year 9% mortgage after 20 years, the monthly interest [portion] is 63%—after 20 years![1]

The following strategies will help you avoid losing money unnecessarily through interest costs and will increase the financial benefits of owning your home.

### Consider Refinancing Your Mortgage

If mortgage interest rates drop by more than two percentage points, it's good to look into refinancing. When you do, take advantage of the savings on interest to get a shorter-term mortgage loan.

### Increase Your Monthly Mortgage Payment

When your mortgage comes up for renewal or on any anniversary, increase the amount of your monthly payment. One of the most effective financial strategies is to renegotiate your mortgage, if possible, to achieve the shortest payment period and the largest monthly payment that you can comfortably afford. Bob, the homeowner introduced earlier, increased his monthly payments by $200, from $805 to $1,005 per month. That simple change will save $67,840 in future interest charges. In addition, Bob will pay off his twenty-five-year mortgage ten years early.

### Make Biweekly Mortgage Payments

Another successful strategy is to request that your bank allow you to make your mortgage payments once every two weeks rather than once a month. Although you are paying virtually the same amount over the year, the fact that half of your payments are applied to the outstanding mortgage two weeks earlier results in substantial savings. In addition, you will pay down your mortgage faster because you'll make the equivalent of one additional full payment every year. (When you pay biweekly, you make twenty-six payments per year, which translates into a month's worth of extra payments during the year.)

For example, Mary has a mortgage of $200,000 at a 5 percent interest rate (renewable every five years) with a twenty-five-year term. The regular mortgage plan called for monthly payments of $1,169.18, which would amount to paying $150,754 in interest over twenty-five years. However, by choosing to make biweekly payments of $584.59, Mary's total interest payments will be $125,523, a savings of $25,231 in interest charges. To see how this would impact your own mortgage, try the mortgage calculator found at Bankrate.com (www.bankrate.com/gookeyword/calc/biweekly-mtg/biweekly.asp).

### *Make Annual Prepayments on Your Mortgage Anniversary*

Another effective strategy is to make an annual prepayment of up to 10 percent of your outstanding mortgage balance on every anniversary of your mortgage. Every dollar of these prepayments will be applied toward the outstanding principal. These prepayments will save tremendously on your future interest charges, allowing you to own your home years ahead of the mortgage's full term. Such prepayments can be made at any time, but the earlier you make the prepayment, the greater the savings. Even a small prepayment in the early years will save a huge amount in future interest payments.

The day you finally pay off your mortgage will be one of the great milestones in your journey toward financial independence. When you make your last mortgage payment, ensure that your lawyer obtains a written statement from your mortgage lender that your mortgage has been paid in full. Your lawyer should also remove the mortgage that is registered against your property in your local title registry office, county clerk's office, or county recorder of deeds office. In some locales you file the needed documents yourself.

### *Renegotiate to Lower Your Mortgage Interest Rate*

Renewing your mortgage is another opportunity to save money. Shop around for the best rates available several months in advance of your renewal date, since it can take a number of weeks to transfer a mortgage to another lender. If you believe interest rates will decline within twelve months, choose a short-term mortgage (six months or a one-year term may be appropriate). Later, when you believe interest rates have reached a low point, lock in these low rates by renewing your mortgage or obtaining a new mortgage.

A generally accepted rule is that you should try to renegotiate your mortgage interest rate if you are paying more than two percentage points higher than the rates currently available and you have more than twenty-four months remaining before your mortgage maturity date. Make certain you understand whatever penalties will be due if you change your mortgage terms. Likewise, if you refinance by taking out a mortgage with a different lender, you will have to pay again for title insurance, closing costs, and sometimes points up front. Those costs will reduce your overall savings.

### *Consider a Variable-Rate Mortgage*

If you have built up substantial equity in your home and have a strong income as well as an investment portfolio, you may realize significant savings by choosing a variable-rate mortgage. A study conducted by Moshe Arye Milevsky of York University found that during the last fifty years a consumer would have paid less in interest by choosing a variable-rate mortgage—compared to a five-year renewable fixed-rate mortgage—a whopping 88.6 percent of the time.[2] Milevsky found that homeowners who chose a fixed-rate mortgage paid a significant interest penalty. The average interest saved by choosing a variable-rate mortgage of $100,000 over a fifteen-year period amounted to an impressive $22,000.[3]

No one can know in advance how far interest rates might rise or fall, so you can never be certain when you should lock in a rate by taking out a fixed-rate mortgage. Since Milevsky's research shows that variable-rate mortgages save on interest charges 88.6 percent of the time, most home-owners should seriously consider a variable-rate mortgage. However, this strategy should be pursued only by those whose income is sufficient to cover increased mortgage payments if interest rates rise quickly.

### Arrange to Own Your Home by the Time You Retire

If you are forty-four years old and have just bought a home with a thirty-year mortgage, you might think you will be paying for that house well into your retirement years. But you can pay off the mortgage before you retire at age sixty-five. Make your mortgage payment every four weeks instead of each month. By doing so, you will pay off the principal at an accelerated rate and will reduce a thirty-year mortgage down to twenty-one years.

### Determine an Approach That Will Generate the Greatest Financial Return

You must decide if it's more beneficial to use available funds to add to the monthly principal payments on your mortgage, or to invest those funds in an outside investment. The decision depends, in part, on your attitude toward financial risk.

If you devote available funds to accelerating your mortgage payoff, the risk is as low as possible. However, if you choose instead to add those funds to outside investments, you are assuming a degree of risk. Can you be reasonably sure that by putting the funds in taxable investments, such as mutual funds or a tax-sheltered individual retirement account (IRA), you will generate *more* after-tax money than the guaranteed savings on interest when you accelerate your mortgage payments?

## YOUR MORTGAGE'S TAX BENEFITS

If you're an American, one of the greatest financial advantages of home mortgages is that you can deduct from your taxable income the annual amount of money you pay in mortgage interest. This provides an enormous benefit for those who own their homes rather than rent. The mortgage-interest deduction can result in a larger tax refund, which then can be applied directly toward the principal of the loan.

## MORTGAGE INSURANCE

It is wise to obtain mortgage life insurance to assure your spouse that, in the event of your premature death, the home you live in will be secured with no additional mortgage payments. The security of a mortgage-free home for your family if you pass away prematurely is one of the greatest gifts you can give. Even if your family chooses to sell the home and move to a smaller property, the elimination of the existing mortgage will provide your family much greater freedom to rearrange their lives.

Part 2

# ACHIEVING FINANCIAL
# INDEPENDENCE

# Chapter 7

# Investments Will Build Your Future

*How to Win by Avoiding Major Losses*

*Money is a terrible master,*
*but an excellent servant.*
—P. T. Barnum

Investing always involves risk, which prevents many people from earning a higher return on their savings. They prefer to play it safe and settle for the low rate of return on government-insured instruments, such as savings bonds or treasury bills. After paying taxes on the income, they are left with little more than their original principal.

But it *is* possible to invest your money to achieve a higher rate of return while minimizing your chances of losing big. You can plan your investments using strategies that will limit your downside risk. In this chapter we will discuss various types of investment options, from certificates of deposit to government bonds to shares of stock to precious metals.

## GOVERNMENT SAVINGS BONDS

One of the safest and easiest choices for very conservative investors is government savings bonds offered by both the U.S. and Canadian governments. Since these savings bonds are backed by the full taxation power of the federal government, and since the government must pay the interest due if it wishes to borrow additional funds in the future, savings bonds are virtually without risk. Government savings bonds can be purchased in various denominations from any major financial institution. Some savings bonds pay regular interest every year while others compound the interest over the duration of the bond. Usually, compound savings bonds provide a higher rate of return.

If you choose to invest in savings bonds, instead of buying one $5,000 bond, for instance, consider buying five $1,000 bonds. This strategy gives you the option of surrendering one or two of the smaller bonds if you need emergency cash, rather than surrendering the whole $5,000 bond.

The government of Israel offers Israel Savings Bonds that provide an excellent guaranteed return for either a five- or ten-year period. The interest rate is usually higher than that of other government bonds because Israel does not pay brokerage commissions. The funds are used to build the infrastructure of Israel, including ports, railways, and desalinization plants that transform salt water into drinkable water. In addition to providing a very high and safe return, these bonds provide an opportunity to support the rebuilding of Israel in a practical way.

## TAX-FREE MUNICIPAL BONDS

Cities raise funds by issuing tax-free municipal bonds, which offer major tax advantages. If the city issuing the bond is in sound financial shape, this can be an excellent way to conservatively invest your funds while earning tax-free interest. You can check on the financial risk for a particular city's tax-free municipal bonds through Standard & Poor's (S&P) or Moody's bond rating service. Ask your broker for a research report and a bond rating. The safest rating available is AAA. Avoid investing in bonds that are rated below an A-minus grade. This type of investment has advantages for any taxpayer in the 28 percent tax bracket or higher because the return on investment is not taxed.

## Treasury Bills

Treasury bills (T-bills) are government-backed investments that are secured by the taxation authority of the federal government and are safe investments as long as the economy is not approaching hyperinflation. When you invest in T-bills, you are lending the government a significant amount of funds for a period of 91, 182, or 364 days at a competitive interest rate. T-bills have the same level of security as government savings bonds but are usually available only in large denominations—$50,000 or more. Rather than paying an interest rate, T-bills are sold to investors at a discount, and the government returns the full face-value amount at maturity. The difference represents your return.

For example, if you purchase a 182-day T-bill for $97,000, six months later the government might pay you $100,000, depending on interest rates. This $3,000 gain (interest) is exempt from state and local taxes for Americans; however, you are subject to federal income tax on these earnings. In the past only wealthy investors were able to purchase Treasury bills. However, recently various stockbrokers started a secondary market in T-bills that allows small investors to invest several thousand dollars in T-bills. You can purchase T-bills from any investment broker, bank, or directly by mail from the Federal Reserve. Since the interest is exempt from state taxes, T-bills are especially advantageous for investors who live in a state that levies high state-income taxes.

## CORPORATE BONDS

Bonds issued by corporations function in the same manner as those issued by governments, except they are not backed by the federal government's taxing authority. The assets of the issuing corporations usually secure corporate bonds. However, it is difficult for the average investor to accurately determine the true financial strength of a corporation from reading its published financial reports and annual reports. In light of the many corporate bond defaults in the last decade and the widespread corporate accounting scandals, I would recommend that you avoid corporate bonds unless you are a professional investor.

## MUTUAL FUNDS AND COMMON STOCKS

More than half of all Americans invest in the stock market. While millions of people own shares directly, the vast majority have placed their money in one of the more than five thousand mutual funds that have sprung up since 1980. Rather than own the shares directly, a mutual-fund investor owns units of the mutual fund. The mutual fund itself actually owns the shares or other investments. When the value of the units of the mutual fund increases due to the rise in value of the underlying stocks and other investments, the owner of the mutual fund benefits. If the mutual fund shares are held in a tax-protected 401(k) plan, an independent retirement account (IRA), or a Roth IRA plan, then the gains are not taxable until they are withdrawn. Details of these tax-sheltered retirement plans are discussed in detail in chapter 12.

If the units of a mutual fund are outside of a tax-sheltered fund, then they are subject to income tax on the gains made during the year, whether or not you have sold your units. First, you will have to pay tax on any gains you make when you sell units of the fund. Second, when the mutual fund itself sells equities it owns at a profit, this creates a capital-gains distribution. The tax on capital gains will be treated differently, depending on whether the gains were short-term profits (twelve months or less) or long-term profits (more than twelve months). Your mutual fund will prepare for each customer a Form 1099-DIV, which will indicate the amount you need to report on your income-tax return. To avoid annual taxation, many investors choose to invest their long-term mutual funds in tax-sheltered plans, such as 401(k)s and IRAs.

Based on the excellent average returns that have been earned by many mutual funds during the last ten years, many investors believe they will automatically achieve great returns and run little risk by continuing to invest in mutual funds. Unfortunately, they are mistaken. Most mutual funds point to their past track record and imply that this is an indication of expected future results. However, as of this writing, the markets are still at an all-time speculative high and are ripe for a crash. Despite the steep correction in prices, the loss of corporate profitability actually causes the current share prices of many equities to remain much higher than prudent investors should pay.

*How to make a million in the stock market? Start with five million!*

In a speculative stock market, it's better for investors to wait until after there is a major drop in the price of shares. As of this writing, average shares are trading at a price-earnings ratio of twenty-two. This means that average share prices are so high it would take twenty-two years to earn enough in dividends to earn back the price you paid for the stock. A normal price-earnings ratio should be between ten and fifteen. To put this in proper perspective, the price-earnings ratio was twenty in the Standard & Poor's 500 Index in the highly speculative period of market peak in 1929 before the crash. Since dividend earnings are so low today compared to the share price, investors are buying inflated stocks at high prices in the vain hope that share prices will go still higher. This is a prescription for disaster. In addition, the stock and bond markets are both threatened by the volatile financial-derivatives market with a staggering two hundred trillion dollars at risk at this time.

The fund managers at many mutual funds have, to a great degree, abandoned the fundamental safeguards that were designed after the 1929 stock market crash. Mutual funds have operated since 1930 under strict investment restrictions that prohibited them from engaging in risky and speculative practices. However, under the competitive pressures of the last decade, many mutual funds have drastically altered the restrictive rules to allow them to pursue highly risky investment strategies.

For example, many mutual funds are speculating unwisely by purchasing securities on margin and selling shares short. Buying on margin occurs when a fund buys equities with borrowed money, using the shares themselves as collateral security. Selling short happens when one borrows a security from a broker and sells it to someone else in the hope that the price will be lower at a later time when you must buy it back and return it to the broker.

Some mutual funds are buying shares for the first time in high-risk companies that are less than three years old. Other funds are speculatively buying shares in other mutual funds rather than making direct investments in the shares of companies. And incredibly, several funds have altered their rules to allow the mutual fund to purchase shares of a company in which officers and trustees of the mutual fund have already personally acquired significant share positions. This leaves the mutual fund open to massive conflicts of interest between the best interests of the individual fund investors and the interests of the managers of the fund.

All of these factors suggest that, at the moment, some mutual funds are not a safe place to put your funds. It is essential that you carefully research the history and reputation of the mutual funds you are interested in. The Internet is an essential tool for research.

When comparing mutual funds, always consider the impact of the management fees the funds charge their customers. Mutual funds declare their annual management fees as a percentage of the total value of the fund and call it their management expense ratio (MER). Often MERs are in the range of 1–2 percent. While these small percentages may seem of little consequence, you need to realize that even a small increase in your fund's MER can cost you many thousands of dollars over twenty or thirty years.

Other investors choose to directly purchase individual equities and stocks issued by American and foreign companies listed on the various stock exchanges. Unless you have the time and inclination to thoroughly research individual stocks, you would be wise to find a certified financial planner (CFP) who can advise you in selecting stocks that are appropriate to your financial situation and to the level of risk you are comfortable with. Your choice of a financial planner is very important, especially if you choose to invest in individual stocks. Be certain that the planner is a certified financial planner.

## MONEY-MARKET FUNDS

These investment funds are a form of mutual fund offered by stockbrokers and various financial institutions. Money-market funds invest your money in short-term financial securities such as T-bills, bonds, or commercial short-term loans offered by large corporations. Instead of owning a bond or T-bill directly, an investor will own a unit in the money-market fund that actually owns the underlying T-bill or bond. Money-market funds calculate the interest generated by the fund's investments on a daily basis.

These funds are very liquid, but they are subject to severe losses when interest rates become volatile. And keep in mind that money-market funds are not protected by the Federal Deposit Insurance Corporation.

The usual minimum investment will be around $1,000, with the earned interest either paid out to the investor every month or reinvested to purchase additional units of the fund. While money-market funds are extremely easy for investors to use, they are quite risky investments at a time of fluctuating interest rates. One of the dangers is that you, as an investor, only own units or shares in the money-market fund. You do not directly own the underlying financial security. If the managers of the money-market fund guess incorrectly regarding the direction of future interest rates, you could lose a substantial portion of your investment. Especially in a day when a number of such funds are taking spectacular risks by investing in the unregulated financial-derivatives market, it may be wise to avoid such funds. Rather than putting your assets into money markets, consider investing directly in whatever investments you judge are appropriate for your portfolio because of their level of risk and possible rate of return.

## TERM DEPOSITS

Term deposits are offered by banks and other financial institutions as a vehicle to invest larger amounts ($5,000 and above) for 90, 180, or 364 days. Term deposits tend to pay less interest than certificates of deposit, but they have the virtue of not being locked in for the full term of the deposit. Term deposits can be surrendered for cash at any time before their maturity date, although you will lose a significant amount of interest that you would otherwise have earned at maturity. However, term deposits issued by strong financial institutions offer excellent security. These are a good, safe place to "park" your investment funds for three to six months while you consider which way the financial market is going before you choose to invest in longer-term investment vehicles.

## CERTIFICATES OF DEPOSIT

Certificates of deposit (CDs) are sold by banks and other large financial institutions as a medium-term investment. The advantage of this vehicle for most investors is the guaranteed rate of compound interest and the higher rate of interest offered for longer-term CDs. The disadvantage is that your funds remain locked in for the duration of a one- to five-year term. (Shorter-term CDs—for three, six, or nine months—usually pay low rates of interest.)

In an emergency, however, you can obtain your money from a one- to five-year CD. As long as the certificate of deposit is transferable, a number of stockbrokers will offer to purchase the CD at a discount prior to its maturity. Certificates of deposit are worthy of consideration when interest rates are high but should probably be avoided if interest rates are low or volatile. Check the business section in your local newspaper for the interest rates being offered by various financial institutions. Before investing in CDs, make sure you verify the financial strength of the bank offering the certificates (see the appendix).

## INVESTMENT PRINCIPLES TO LIMIT YOUR RISK OF LOSS

Strangely, many people research buying a home more than they educate themselves regarding possible investments. But you can't achieve financial independence unless you invest the time to research the most appropriate investments and the best approaches to investing. For example, with a little research you will learn that you can cut your losses by using strategies such as stop-loss orders and trading stops. Stop-loss orders instruct your broker to sell your investment immediately if the price drops to a certain point that you have determined in advance. Plan your investments with strategies that limit your downside risk. You cannot afford to endure a major hit that wipes out years of financial growth.

### Plan Your Strategy with Diversification

Many people choose their investments in a random fashion based on the latest information and tips they receive from friends, newspapers, television, the Internet, or investment magazines. In the absence of a strategic plan, they end up with a number of different investment vehicles that are unrelated to any logical investment plan.

It's far better to choose the most appropriate portfolio based on which asset classes will help you reach your long-term financial goals. Then, within your chosen portfolio, you should select particular investments that will achieve your goals with appropriate diversification to protect against undue loss. For instance, if you are knowledgeable about the health-services industry, it might make sense to choose a combination of stocks in health-related corporations, pharmaceuticals, and municipal bonds related to hospital construction. As a matter of principle, however, avoid even high-performing stocks if they are connected with gambling, tobacco, alcohol, pornography, or companies involved in child labor overseas.

Since no one can know in advance which asset class will rise and which will fall in a particular time period, it's best to spread your investments among different classes. The wisest man who ever lived, King Solomon, favored such diversity of investments. He wrote, "Cast thy bread upon the waters: for thou shalt find it after many days. Give a portion to seven, and also to eight; for thou knowest not what evil shall be upon the earth" (Ecclesiastes 11:1–2).

## *Use Mutual Funds to Achieve Diversification*

Unless you are a professional investor, you should choose a mutual fund over individual stocks. Choose a no-load mutual fund with low expense ratios. A no-load fund does not charge a sales fee to its customers. An expense ratio is the percentage (%) of the fund assets that is charged to the client to cover operating expenses, management fees, and administrative fees, excluding brokerage costs. As a fund increases its assets, the expense ratio normally decreases. Carefully research the mutual fund's five- and ten-year historical returns. Many Internet sites provide excellent charts and comparison reports that track thousands of mutual funds. Many investors choose index funds that track the results of the entire stock market to reduce the risks associated with individual stocks. An index fund is one that replicates the performance of a particular sector, such as the Standard & Poor's 500 Index.

As you research mutual funds on the Internet, you can check the types of shares that the fund holds. For instance, does the fund hold shares in tobacco, alcohol, so-called "reproductive health services," casinos, and so on?

## *Don't Expect to Duplicate the Returns of Past Years*

It is a well-known axiom: past performance is not a guarantee of future results. Yet millions of investors continue to believe that their future stock price results will parallel the results of the last decade. The incredible gains in stock prices during the 1990s were very unusual and are unlikely to occur again in our lifetimes.

One survey of investors in 1999 revealed that they anticipated stock market returns would average approximately 19 percent annually during the next decade. However, records reveal that annualized stock market returns averaged 11 percent over the last seventy-five years. If you choose a particular investment based on its past excellent performance, you would be wise to limit your amount in this investment to just a portion of your diversified portfolio.

### Evaluate the Real Cost of Your Investments

Unfortunately, most investors give little thought to the total cost of the investment fees and commissions associated with most investment vehicles. Many believe that investment commissions will not significantly affect their returns if their stocks or mutual funds perform well. However, stock-broker commissions and mutual-fund management fees can significantly reduce your ultimate investment returns. For example, if your cost of investing amounts to 2 percent annually in fees or commissions, then a 10 percent annual average gross return on your investments will be reduced to an 8 percent net return. On a ten-year investment of $100,000, the 2 percent investment fee will reduce your final return by $43,482—a very significant reduction.

Many are tempted to invest with companies on the Internet, such as E*TRADE (www.etrade.com), so they can save the brokerage fees. However, the casual investor who has not done significant research can lose his entire investment by making unwise decisions.

### Avoid Holding On Until You Win It Back

When people have several investments that have increased significantly and others that have dropped in value, they tend to sell the stocks or mutual funds that have gained rather than those that have lost. Many investors are reluctant to admit that the stock they chose has resulted in a loss. Therefore, rather than sell a losing stock, they hold on to it, hoping it will eventually rebound.

Studies have indicated, however, that selling the winners and holding the losers is usually unwise. Terrance Odean, a finance professor at the University of California, examined the stock-trading patterns of investors over a seven-year period. He discovered that investors were approximately 50 percent more likely to sell stocks that had gained in value than stocks that had lost value. His study also revealed that the winning stocks outperformed the losing stocks by 3.5 percent in the two-year period after their sale.[1] Therefore, you should consider selling the investments that have lost money and reinvest in your winning investments.

Don't abandon an investment based on emotion. The decision to hold or sell an investment should be based on your careful evaluation of its future prospects rather than on its current day-to-day performance.

## Avoid Excessive Trading

We are inundated with financial information from the Internet, television, radio, newspapers, and magazines. As a result, many people believe they can choose the winners and avoid the losers. One problem with this active trading strategy is the adverse effect on your investment returns due to the cost of additional commissions. A study by Terrance Odean and Brad Barber looked at the trading results of 66,000 investors with a large discount brokerage house. They found that the 20 percent of investors who were the least active in trading stocks achieved 5.5 percent greater annual returns than the 20 percent who traded most actively.[2] The lesson is clear: buy quality investments and hold them. Let time and compound returns work for you to produce financial success.

## Take the Long-Term Approach

Wise investors carefully make their investment choices and then let time and the growth in the economy produce the return they desire. It is usually a mistake to analyze your investment returns every day. Unless extraordinary events are occurring, it is usually best to seriously analyze your investment portfolio once or twice a year. At those times, if market conditions dictate, you can make any needed adjustments.

## A Prudent Portfolio

I believe we are at risk of a major stock and bond market correction that could wipe out a significant part of the life savings of millions of investors. Unless you are a professional investor, I strongly recommend that you consider transferring your existing investment in only stocks or a few mutual funds into a more conservative and secure portfolio, such as a mix of large, well-known companies and several mutual funds with an excellent long-term track record, money-market funds with a strong multiyear return, Treasury bills, and certificates of deposit. Keep your funds in these more secure instruments until a stock market correction restores stock values to a more realistic valuation. After the stock market drops, there will be excellent opportunities for investors who have avoided major losses. Prudent investors with cash will be able to purchase shares in solid corporations and conservative mutual funds at a fraction of the cost of these shares before the market correction.

## Your Inflation–Interest Rate Strategy

If the bank's prime lending rate (the rate charged to its best customers) has risen more than a few percentage points in six months, it is a good indication that we are entering a period of high interest and high inflation. In such a situation, consider placing your money in shorter-term investment vehicles such as T-bills or short-term deposits at a strong bank at the highest interest rate available. As they mature, you should keep renewing them as interest rates continue rising. Then, when you believe that interest rates have peaked, transfer your funds into the highest interest long-term investment available, such as a certificate of deposit issued by a very strong bank. This strategy will lock in high-interest rates for a number of years.

## THE RISK OF HYPERINFLATION

There is a growing danger of hyperinflation in North America as our governments finally hit the wall financially after decades of irresponsible borrowing. In the United States, the national debt has grown to more than $7 trillion, and the compounding interest on that debt is growing at an astounding rate. The United States is running annual deficits ($420 billion in 2004), and it is impossible to run extraordinary deficits year after year without eventually triggering massive inflation. Some economists have calculated that the total federal tax revenues in the United States will be insufficient to pay the interest on our national debt within several decades. At that point, the government will be forced to hyperinflate the currency as the only practical method to produce the needed additional funds to pay for social services, interest charges on the national debt, and the enormous daily cost of government and national defense.

The warning signs will be apparent for several years before the final inflationary crisis hits. We will witness growing wage demands, rapidly rising prices, large swings in stock prices, a declining value of U.S. currency against the stronger Japanese yen and the euro, and continued astronomical federal government deficits.

Hyperinflation will significantly damage the economies of the United States and Canada, as it did many national economies in the twentieth century. Following World War I, the Weimar Republic of Germany experienced the financial nightmare of raging inflation from 1918 to 1923, and it completely destroyed the life savings of the German people. Prices rose astronomically, and millions lost jobs, setting the stage for the rise of Adolf Hitler. In 1918 a pound of butter cost one German mark. By 1923 an identical pound of butter cost hundreds of millions of marks. People used wheelbarrows to carry the enormous stacks of paper currency needed to buy groceries. Factories were forced to pay their workers every two to three hours and let them off work to quickly buy food before the newly printed marks became worthless. In 1923 a 100-million-mark German bank note would not cover the cost of lunch!

Since then, other sophisticated economies—including Brazil, Argentina, Chile, and Russia—have experienced catastrophic periods of hyperinflation. Argentina was one of the world's strongest economies in the first decade of the 1900s. However, since World War I, the currencies of Argentina, Brazil, and Chile have devalued until today they are worth less than 0.1 percent of their currency value in 1915.

During a period of hyperinflation, the stock market will become quite volatile as inflation surges higher. Mutual funds and stocks should be avoided during hyperinflation by all but those who have the strongest nerves. Even with hyperinflation, however, there are survival strategies that will benefit the prudent investor.

If you see events leading toward hyperinflation, liquidate your fixed long-term assets. Unfortunately, you may have to pay substantial surrender charges. But in a time of hyperinflation, if you hold on to your long-term investments in bonds, pensions, annuities, and fixed-income funds, they may become virtually worthless.

Then consider transferring your cash into precious metals, stable foreign currencies, and other conservative investments in countries that are not yet experiencing hyperinflation. Increase your investment in precious metals—either in bullion bars, bullion coins, or precious metals mutual funds—from the typical 10 percent to as much as 35 percent of your investment assets. In hyperinflationary times, the rest of your portfolio should include real estate, foreign investments, and strong foreign currencies that are backed by gold. As one example, the Swiss franc is fully backed by gold and is therefore an extremely strong and stable currency. An investment in a Swiss franc bank account, annuity, or bond, while paying a relatively conservative interest rate, will provide security from the dangers you will face in times of hyperinflation.

Even after a disastrous period of hyperinflation, the crisis will someday end, and financial stability will return. Those who have avoided serious losses and retained their assets and cash will be in a position to purchase quality financial investments at phenomenal discounts.

## GOLD AND SILVER: A CONSERVATIVE FINANCIAL STRATEGY

Gold possesses a number of important characteristics that make it one of the best investments available to preserve monetary values. Over the centuries gold has retained an almost constant value. As a result, prudent people have relied on gold as a wise long-term investment and the ultimate safeguard for their assets.

Gold does not tarnish, corrode, or rust, which makes it a vital metal for industrial, medical, and complex high-tech applications. Because gold can transmit an electrical current in extremely low and high temperatures, it serves as a vital electrical connector in sophisticated supercomputers, the space shuttle, and advanced telecommunications. As the most ductile and malleable metal on earth, a single ounce of gold could actually be extended into a wire fifty miles long.

The entire amount of gold produced from mines since the beginning of recorded history amounts to approximately 120,000 metric tons. The total global hoard of gold today would occupy a single cube only sixty feet by sixty feet by sixty feet. The world's total holdings of gold could be transported in a single ship with the value of approximately $1.4 trillion.

The chairman of the U.S. Federal Reserve System, Alan Greenspan, told Congress in February 1994, "Gold is a different type of commodity because virtually all of the gold that has ever been produced still exists." He continued, "Therefore changes in the level of production have very little effect on the ongoing price, which means that it's virtually wholly a monetary demand phenomenon. It's a store of value measure which has shown a fairly consistent lead on inflation expectations, and has been over the years a reasonably good indicator. It does this better than commodity prices or a lot of other things."[3] Greenspan also stated in 1966, "In the absence of the gold standard, there is no way to protect savings from confiscation through inflation."[4]

This is a rather amazing admission about the value of gold from the world's most respected international banker! The inflationary monetary expansion created by the Federal Reserve during the last two decades virtually guarantees that we will face massive increases in inflation in the years ahead. If that occurs, the price of gold and silver is likely to rise substantially. Investing in gold and silver should form a small but significant part of a balanced, long-term investment strategy. Gold should not be considered as a speculative investment for quick profits but rather as a secure part of your long-term investment strategy.

Following the Revolutionary War, the U.S. Congress adopted a bimetallic standard (both gold and silver) for backing America's new currency. Congress set the price of gold at $19.30 per ounce, which continued basically unchanged for forty-two years. In 1834 the gold price was raised to $20.67, and this price continued in force for a century. However, in 1934 President Franklin D. Roosevelt raised gold to $35 an ounce. The 1971 Smithsonian Agreement increased the price to $38 an ounce. However, two years later the U.S. Treasury devalued the dollar further and raised the price of gold to $42.22 an ounce. Finally a decision was made by the major nations throughout the world to allow all international currencies to float freely against the price of gold and find their own appropriate level. By mid-1973 the price of gold exploded to $120 an ounce.

Speculation on the rapidly rising price of gold ultimately produced an explosion that resulted in gold prices reaching an unprecedented $850 an ounce at its peak on January 21, 1980. Obviously, the speculators had over-reached themselves, and that price could not be sustained. From 1980 until 1993 gold experienced a thirteen-year downtrend as its price dropped to $347.50. As of this writing, the price of gold has risen to well over $440 an ounce.

> *If all the gold in the world were melted down into a solid cube it would be about the size of an eight room house. If a man got possession of all that gold— billions of dollars worth—he could not buy a friend, character, peace of mind, clear conscience or a sense of eternity.*
> —*Charles F. Bunning*

### Gold Investment Strategies

If the price of gold or silver begins to climb, don't shift too much of your portfolio into precious metals assuming that the rise in value will continue. Instead, consider investing *over the long term* in precious metals as a significant part of a balanced portfolio. Gold and silver investments should form between 10 and 15 percent of your normal investment portfolio while interest rates and inflation are low.

The basic rationale for placing some of your investment funds in gold and silver is simply prudence and insurance against risk. For thousands of years, gold and silver have remained the most stable and universally accepted medium of exchange. In the early 1920s you could buy a good quality man's suit with an ounce of gold. Despite the massive financial changes and political upheavals during the last eighty-five or more years, an ounce of gold will still buy a good man's suit. Unlike U.S. paper currency, which is subject to devaluation by government-produced inflation, gold and silver remain in limited quantity, so they can never lose their true value. In the event of hyperinflation, an investment in gold and silver will provide significant protection. In the case of a complete financial collapse, the investor who wisely purchased precious metals in the form of gold and silver coins, bullion, or a mutual fund invested in precious metals will retain significant purchasing power while many other investors will be left with increasingly worthless currency.

Aside from a 10–15 percent investment in precious metals as a normal investment strategy, you should seriously consider increasing your investments in gold and silver if you see indications of severe economic problems ahead or if you see inflation beginning to rise quickly. In my opinion, in the next decades the U.S. government will find that the growing national debt load will force the government to spend almost all of the taxes raised to pay the interest on this immense debt. At the point when international borrowing becomes extremely difficult for the government, the U.S. Treasury will begin to secretly hyperinflate the currency as the only practical policy it can follow. In this economic scenario, the rate of inflation will eventually skyrocket beyond anything ever experienced in North American history.

### Semi-numismatic Gold Coins

In 1935 President Roosevelt made the possession of gold bullion by Americans illegal, but citizens could still own semi-numismatic gold coins because these coins were legal tender. These coins have collector value because of their relative rarity. Even though possessing gold bullion is no longer illegal, many financial planners believe that prudent American investors should still hold some of their gold in the form of semi-numismatic coins rather than solely as gold bullion coins and bars because of the unfortunate experience of bullion confiscation during the Great Depression. The price of high-quality semi-numismatic coins has risen more quickly in the last decade than gold and silver bullion. I highly recommend a book that explores investment in semi-numismatic coins entitled *Rediscovering Gold in the 21st Century* by Craig R. Smith.

## Bullion Coins

President Gerald Ford introduced a law in 1974 that finally made possession of gold bullion legal for all Americans. Those who choose to invest in gold bullion can now purchase it in small units, bars, or wafers in various sizes, with the advantage of instant liquidity and universal negotiability. Since there is a small charge for each bar in addition to the price of the actual gold, it is to your advantage to buy the largest bar you can afford. Make certain that the gold bar is stamped by a reputable refiner such as Johnson Matthey or Handy & Harman, which will guarantee its purity (usually .9999 fine).

Avoid any newspaper or mail advertisements selling gold or silver. Thousands of naive investors have lost their money when they sent in checks and never received the promised gold. Purchase your gold from a large, internationally recognized dealer or well-known bank after shopping for the lowest commission and bar charges. Depending on the state or province you live in, you may have to pay sales tax on your gold purchases. A safety-deposit box in your local bank is recommended for the safe storing of any precious metal investments. Remember that the cost of the safety-deposit box is also a tax-deductible expense.

Many investors prefer gold or silver coins because of their portability, universal liquidity, and negotiability. Recommended one-ounce gold coins include the Canadian Maple Leaf, the South African Krugerrand, and the American Eagle. In addition to the price of the gold, the coin's price will usually include a premium of 10 percent or more for a one-tenth-of-an-ounce coin, while a one-ounce coin will usually bear only a 3.5 percent premium. When you resell these gold coins, you will normally recover some portion of the premium. (Protect your gold and silver coins from scratches that would reduce their value to a future purchaser.)

It is generally unwise to leave your gold or silver investment in the possession of the seller in return for a certificate. Wise investors demand physical delivery of the bullion or coins. Insist that you possess the gold and silver directly rather than accepting paper documentation only.

The secret to financial success in the precious metals market is simple: buy low and sell high. Everyone knows the rule, but few investors actually follow it. Most people end up following a different principle: buy high and sell low. The public was generally not interested in buying gold when it was available at only $35 an ounce. However, when the price reached market highs of $800–$850 an ounce, the public rushed to buy. But by that point it is already far too late to buy gold wisely. The intent of these late buyers was to "buy high but sell even higher." This practice usually ends in disaster, as people tend to purchase their gold at its market peak just as the price begins to drop.

Today, however, a number of factors indicate that the price of gold will rise substantially. We have already explored the growing dangers of inflation and its impact on gold prices. Second, market demand for gold is growing substantially. After a half century of the Chinese government forbidding its citizens to own gold, 1.3 billion Chinese are now able to own gold legally. For more than a thousand years, the Islamic world used the gold dinar. However, in 1924 Turkey ceased to mint this coin. In 2003 Malaysia began to mint a new one-ounce gold dinar coin. Islamic financial and theological leaders have suggested that Muslims should use the dinar as currency and that Islamic nations should use gold in international trade. Since new gold production cannot match current global demand, the price of gold will most likely rise.

As you make investment decisions, don't get carried away by media and market hype. Remember, everything changes. While the majority of investors act as though either a recession or a boom will continue forever, they are always wrong. Recessions always end, and all market booms eventually crash. Consider purchasing gold and silver as a form of financial insurance policy rather than as a speculative investment. Investing in precious metals should be part of your long-term strategy in both good times and bad.

# Chapter 8

# Protect Yourself Against Fraud

*Don't Let Scams Endanger Your Wealth*

*It requires a great deal of boldness*
*and a great deal of caution to make a*
*great fortune, and when you have it,*
*it requires ten times as much skill to keep it.*
—Ralph Waldo Emerson

A very real threat to your goal of financial freedom is one you might not even think about—having your money stolen through fraud. The number of thieves who are planning ways to get their hands on your money is increasing. And they are employing more sophisticated methods than ever before.

You will be approached with get-rich-quick schemes on the Internet as well as by mail, e-mail, telephone, and even in your social circles. Whenever someone promises you a fabulous return on your investment, the likelihood is that you will lose your shirt if you choose to invest. If someone approaches you about some financial scheme, consult an accountant or financial advisor, or do your own research to see if it is a genuine opportunity. Odds are, it will be a scam. A good rule of thumb: if it sounds too good to be true, it is too good to be true.

Your plan for financial success needs to be supported by a strong awareness of the individuals, groups, and companies that develop schemes to take what you have worked so hard to gain. After you read this chapter, discuss it with members of your family, especially older parents, who are often the target of predators. The book of Proverbs warns us that "he that maketh haste to be rich shall not be innocent" (28:20).

## PROTECT YOUR CREDIT CARDS

One real threat to your finances is thieves who attempt to steal your credit-card information. Here are some ideas to protect your credit cards.

1. Never leave credit cards in the glove compartment of your vehicle. Every year thousands of people have their credit cards stolen from their cars, making it easy for thieves to run up their credit-card charges and engage in identity theft.

2. Buy an inexpensive paper shredder to destroy your financial documents and credit-card receipts. Never place unshredded financial documents in the trash, where thieves can find them.

3. Whenever you change your address, immediately notify everyone you deal with financially (banks, credit-card companies, utilities). Be sure to notify your post office to make certain that financial mail does not fall into the hands of thieves. Many Americans have suffered identity theft after their mail was delivered to a former address.

4. Carefully examine credit-card and bank statements every month to make certain no one is using your credit information to defraud you. If you notice unauthorized charges, notify your bank or credit-card company immediately.

In the last decade, credit-card companies have begun using sophisticated computer programs to watch for any deviation in their clients' credit-card usage. When the computer program detects a significant deviation, a representative of the credit-card company will call either the client or the store where a purchase is being made to verify that it is an authorized use of the credit card. A few years ago Kaye and I were traveling in England, and Visa contacted us through our office to ask whether we had used our credit card to purchase several fur coats in Toronto. As soon as we confirmed that we had not made these purchases, they immediately refused the transaction, cancelled our credit card, and replaced it the same day with a new card and a new account number.

If a credit card is stolen and used to make purchases, banks and credit-issuing companies assume the financial risk for such misuse as long as the customer provides timely notice. Once you become aware of the loss of a wallet or purse containing credit and debit cards, immediately notify the affected credit and financial institutions. Most banks will arrange to immediately provide replacement credit or debit cards with new PIN numbers.

5. When using an automatic teller machine (ATM) to access cash, make deposits, or get account information, be aware of your surroundings and block any neighboring customers' views when you input your PIN. Never carry your PIN in your wallet, and avoid using an easily guessed number such as one based on an address or a birth date.

## Fraud That Arrives over the Telephone

While numerous legitimate companies and charities solicit consumers through phone calls, con artists also use the phone. Dishonest telemarketers understand that it is human nature to want to believe we can get rich quick. However, the Word of God warns us against the temptation of greed: "A faithful man shall abound with blessings: but he that maketh haste to be rich shall not be innocent" (Proverbs 28:20).

Older Americans are the most vulnerable to telephone fraud, because they are the most likely to be home to receive phone calls. They often are too polite to hang up on unwanted solicitors, and they usually have disposable income and savings.

When you receive a phone call marketing any product or service, determine the identity of the party before you consider making a financial commitment. You should always check out the identity and reputation of unfamiliar charities or companies with your local Better Business Bureau (BBB) and your state's consumer agency. You can locate the phone number of your state's consumer agency in the government section of the phone book.

Be aware that fraudulent companies frequently close down a company or charity and then quickly open a new one with a slightly different name to avoid being identified as a group that should be avoided. Therefore, even if there are no fraudulent complaints on file, it does not mean the companies are definitely legitimate. Also be aware that it is a common practice of fraudulent groups to use a slight variation of a well-known charity's name. As a general rule, I recommend that you avoid doing business with charities or companies that approach you by phone, because it is virtually impossible to check them out properly.

In addition, be wary of groups that claim to be raising money for a police officers' or firefighters' charity. The caller is probably working for a fund-raising company that retains as much as 85 percent of the funds raised. There are also many dishonest fund-raisers who use the phone to raise money that will never be used for a legitimate charitable purpose. Since there are tens of thousands of legitimate charities that you can check out (especially religious charities associated with your church), it does not make good financial sense to give money to strangers representing an unknown charity. My wife and I have a policy of donating all gifts through our church so we know exactly where the funds are going.

It is valuable to obtain and use caller ID to verify the identity of those who are calling and to screen calls you prefer not to take. When you do choose to purchase products or services over the phone, it is wise to pay with a credit card. Unlike payments with checks, money orders, or cash, a credit-card payment allows you to dispute the credit-card charge with Visa or MasterCard if the transaction proves unsatisfactory.

### Your "Do Not Call" Rights

Fortunately, Congress has passed legislation to protect consumers against unwanted telemarketing calls. You can add your phone number to the national Do Not Call Registry either by calling 888-382-1222 or entering your phone number on the Do Not Call Web site: www.donotcall.gov. This action should stop the vast majority of unwanted marketing calls. However, if you still receive telemarketing calls, report these violations of the law at www.donotcall.gov or by calling 888-382-1222.

### Warning Signs to Watch For

Whenever dishonest individuals practice phone fraud, they engage in telltale practices that are illegal. For example, solicitors cannot legally request up-front fees in return for promises that they will secure loans or credit cards for you or that they will correct or repair your credit rating. Also, beware of those who claim that your payment of a requested amount of money will enable you to qualify to win some prize.

You should be alert for a variety of signs that strongly indicate the possibility of fraud:

- a request that you give them your bank-account number or credit-card number, even though you are not buying a product or service
- refusal to send you written information regarding their offer
- any pressure or threat of immediate price increases if you fail to act today
- a demand that you send money by courier
- a demand that you pay money for taxes, customs fees, and so forth in order to receive a prize
- a request that you pay someone a fee to have them recover money you lost in previous frauds
- a refusal to accept your demand that they cease calling you (Do not hesitate to hang up on a caller if you are not interested in his or her offer.)
- any telephone solicitation that originates from outside the country (It is very difficult to track down and prosecute fraudulent activities that are beyond U.S. jurisdiction. If you are asked to deal with a foreign company, be very cautious about the possibility of fraud.)

Sometimes dishonest people call and claim to be an employee of your bank or another company you do business with. They request that you confirm or update the personal information in your file. Refuse to give confidential financial information to anyone who calls, regardless of what company or government agency they claim to represent. You should contact the company or government agency directly to verify whom you are dealing with before providing personal or financial information.

### Telephone Cramming

A relatively new type of telephone fraud is known as telephone cramming. While in the past only telephone charges appeared on your monthly phone bill, today it's possible to charge a wide variety of services and products to your telephone account. Other companies can bill you through your phone account for services as diverse as Internet services, call paging, voice mail, caller ID, or club membership fees. The telephone company agrees to bill its customers for these services and pass on the agreed amount to the other companies. However, when a dishonest company attempts to add charges to your telephone account for services you have never agreed to purchase, it is called cramming.

With this in mind, always be cautious about signing product coupons and contest entry forms, because the fine print might include your unwitting agreement to purchase a product or service whose charges will appear on your next phone statement. Another dishonest marketing ploy involves sending out junk mail that contains a negative option, which means that unless you send back a written notice refusing the service or product, the company will assume you have agreed to the promotion and will charge the cost to your phone account. Scrutinize every phone bill to verify that all of the phone calls and extraneous charges are legitimate. You are not responsible for charges you did not authorize. However, you must contact the phone company and dispute the charge.

If you have repeated problems with unauthorized charges being added to your phone account, ask your telephone company to block any future billing of nontelephone charges from outside companies.

## CREDIT-REPAIR FRAUDS

Ads offering credit repair appear on the Internet, in newspapers, and in the yellow pages. These ads boldly proclaim that they will clean up the negative credit report that is preventing you from obtaining loans or credit cards. However, no company can eliminate negative information from your credit report if that information is accurate. The only type of information that can be removed or changed is information that can be demonstrated to be incorrect. And you can correct inaccurate data yourself by contacting the three national credit-reporting agencies.

By federal law, you can obtain a free copy of your credit report once a year. It's wise to request a copy from each of the three major credit-reporting agencies: Equifax, 800-685-1111, www.equifax.com; Experian, 888-397-3742, www.experian.com; and TransUnion, 800-888-4213, www.transunion.com.

When you receive your credit report, it will contain instructions on how to dispute any inaccurate information in your file. There is no cost to you to attempt to correct the data in your report. If you had trouble in the past paying a bill, you may add a short note to your file explaining the reason (disability, job loss, a legal dispute, etc.).

> *Another good thing about being poor is that when you are seventy your children will not have you declared legally insane in order to gain control of your estate.*
> —Woody Allen

It is illegal for credit-repair services to request payment until they have fulfilled their promises. Legally credit-repair services must provide their customers with an explanation of customers' legal rights along with a detailed written contract. You have three days in which you may cancel your contract with a for-profit credit-repair service. Occasionally credit-repair companies will suggest that you create a new credit file, in a practice known as "file segregation," to escape your bad credit history through the use of a new tax identification number and a different Social Security number. This is illegal. The best advice is to avoid credit-repair agencies altogether.

It is far wiser to get help from agencies such as a local Consumer Credit

Counseling Service (CCCS), which can work with you and your creditors to arrange a new payment plan to facilitate the timely payment of your outstanding loans and the improvement of your credit record. You can locate the nearest Consumer Credit Counseling Service toll-free at 800-388-2227 or at www.nfcc.org.

## INVESTMENT FRAUD SCHEMES

If a representative of an unknown company invites you to invest in any scheme or "opportunity," turn it down. Many of these offers are presented as having no risk. But *all* investments have a risk element that needs to be investigated thoroughly before you invest. A large number of e-mail offers for investments are fraudulent, so it is wise to avoid this type of offer altogether.

Always demand that a company present its proposal in writing. Once you receive a written proposal, if you don't understand every detail and the risk associated with the investment, refuse to get involved. Also, any pressure to invest immediately is a warning sign of the probability of fraud. Another warning sign is the promise that you will make large profits in a short period of time. *No one* can predict in advance how well any particular investment will do.

After a lifetime involved with investments, both professionally as a financial planner and personally as an active investor, I offer the following cautions:

- Avoid investments in commodities such as oil, copper, art, and precious metals unless you have done detailed research and have enough experience and assets, and you are willing to sustain serious losses. The vast majority of those who have invested in commodities have lost a great deal of their investments.

- Pay no attention to investment advice, tips, or testimonials from people you do not know.
- Avoid any offer to invest in offshore investments that are promoted on the basis of saving taxes. In addition to the investment being outside the jurisdiction of American authorities should this be a fraud, you will still be liable for income taxes. Since September 11, 2001, the Treasury Department and the IRS have been tracking all flows of funds into and out of the country. Your investment in any offshore concern will flag your file for an audit to ensure that you are paying the taxes due and that you are not involved in money laundering.
- Research all questionable investment offers by checking with the following agencies: your state securities regulator; the U.S. Securities and Exchange Commission, 800-732-0330, www.sec.gov; the North American Securities Administrators Association, 202-737-0900, www.nasaa.org. For information on commodities, check with the National Futures Association, 800-621-3570, www.nfa.futures.org.

## INTERNET FRAUD

While the Internet has been a tremendous advance in communications and the best research tool in history, it is also the best tool ever created to facilitate crime, especially fraud against consumers. Electronic commerce on the Internet continues to grow at an astonishing rate. Jupiter Research estimated in the spring of 2003 that sales on the Internet would surpass $90 billion in 2003 and grow to more than $133 billion by 2005.[1] We need to be wise in protecting ourselves from consumer fraud and identity theft while using this remarkable tool.

As the following figures indicate, the Internet is a dangerous place for unwary consumers. However, there are ways to minimize your exposure to identity theft and fraud while surfing the Internet.

## INTERNET FRAUD STATISTICS

Internet fraud in the period January–June 2004
Average Loss: $803

**Top 10 Frauds**

| | |
|---|---|
| Online auctions | 28% |
| General merchandise | 19% |
| Nigerian money offers | 9% |
| Phishing (identity theft) | 5% |
| Information/adult services | 3% |
| Lotteries/lottery clubs | 2% |
| Fake-check scams | 2% |
| Computer equipment/software | 1% |
| Fake-escrow services | 1% |
| Internet access services | 1%[2] |

### *Shopping Safely on the Internet*

1. Carefully research any company that you intend to do business with over the Internet.

2. Whenever you shop on the Internet, use your credit card. This will enable you to refuse to pay for defective or unwanted goods or services by reporting the transaction to your credit-card company.

3. Carefully examine all features of an item offered on the Internet: total price, shipping costs, delivery times, warranty, complaint process, and return policy.

4. Always print out and keep on file the information regarding your purchase in case a dispute arises.

5. Never submit sensitive financial information—such as bank-account or credit-card numbers—by e-mail. Any information in e-mail messages is vulnerable to hackers.

6. When you submit sensitive financial information to a trusted Web site, the "http" at the beginning of the URL address bar in your Internet browser should change to "https" or "shttp," indicating a secure transaction. If it does not, immediately stop the transaction since any hacker could gain access to this information.

7. If you intend to use the Internet to purchase a large number of items in the foreseeable future, consider obtaining a controlled payment number, which is a safe and effective method to protect your real credit-card number and prevent identity theft while shopping online. Controlled payment numbers issued by companies such as Orbiscom allow you, as a registered customer, to obtain a unique number (linked to your actual credit-card account number) so you can buy services or products online without revealing your credit-card information. Once registered, you can access the controlled payment number directly from your issuing bank's Web site. To explore this option, visit Orbiscom's Web site, www.orbiscom.com, or research any other company, such as Discover Card, offering this secure Internet payment service.

### Nigerian Letters or Money Schemes

Virtually every investor, professional, or businessperson has been approached by letter, fax, or e-mail by an unknown individual who claims to be a banker, government official, or spouse of a government official in Nigeria. This individual claims he or she wants to send you millions of dollars to assist himself or herself in accessing funds in Africa. These schemes are known as "Nigerian letters," or 419 scams (from the 419 provision in the Nigerian penal code). A typical 419 scam message looks something like this:

Dear Sir,

I am pleased to propose a confidential business transaction to our mutual benefit. I and my colleagues in the Nigerian government possess legal instruments to transfer the sum of $45,000,000.00 into a foreign company's account in our mutual favor. This amount is the result of an overinvoiced contract, executed, commissioned, and paid for three years ago by a foreign contractor. We are seeking your assistance to transfer these funds to your account as our procedures require that they only can be remitted to a foreign bank account. As civil servants, we are forbidden to operate foreign bank accounts. The total sum of $45,000,000.00 will be shared as follows:

25 percent to the foreign-bank-account holder (you)

65 percent for us

10 percent to settle any incidental expenses

We shall commence the transfer of funds to you as soon as you send the following documents and information through the above fax number:

1. Three copies of your company's letterhead and invoice papers signed and stamped

2. Your banker's name, address, and fax number

3. The account number and name of your beneficiary

Keep in mind that this is an absolutely private and personal deal, nonofficial, and should be treated with all measures of secrecy and confidentiality.

If you are foolish and greedy enough to fall for this scam, you will be asked to send significant funds for various taxes as well as transfer and transaction costs. The people behind this fraud know how to appeal to the investor's greed by promising that the North American partner will obtain millions of dollars as a commission for assisting the Nigerian officials to access the funds they claim are "locked up" due to legal or banking problems. They will ask you to provide your bank-account numbers to facilitate the sending of these huge funds to your bank.

To gain the victim's trust, they sometimes actually send an advance commission by check with a demand that the victim immediately wire them money for the taxes and fees associated with the transaction. After the victim wires the money, he ruefully discovers that the commission check bounces. Thousands of Americans have lost thousands of dollars in fees, taxes, charges, and the illegal accessing of their bank accounts.

Never respond to these offers. Even though the Nigerian con men know that millions have read 419 warnings, they continue to send spam e-mails every day to every e-mail address they can obtain. They know they can profit from greed if only one person in a million responds.

### Identity-Theft Schemes

Every year almost ten million people become new victims of identity theft. The Federal Trade Commission estimates that the average victim will spend between fourteen and sixteen months clearing up the identity confusion and resulting credit problems. In addition, the average identity-theft victim will spend as much as 175 hours and more than $1,000 to clear his name. This new crime is a growing threat to your goal of achieving financial independence.

The act of attempting to steal your identity is called "phishing." One of the most commonly used techniques is for criminals to pretend to be representatives of your bank, a store, or a government agency. They ask you to confirm your confidential account information, saying that they need it due to computer problems or some other reason. Another devious technique is to impersonate representatives of the fraud department of a company that you deal with and suggest that they need to confirm your personal data to defend you *against* identity theft. A novel deception is to call the victim and claim to represent a lottery. They say they need your personal data, including your bank-account number, so they can deposit your lottery winnings directly into your account. You should never respond to such requests.

Beware of any unsolicited e-mail message that instructs you to click on a link to a Web site. Often it's a fraudulent site that impersonates the genuine Web site of a familiar company or government agency. These e-mails are very convincing, but if you fill in the requested information, your personal and financial data will be in the hands of crooks, who will be able to access your bank accounts as well as apply for credit or loans in your name.

Similarly, if someone contacts you and claims to represent your bank or a company you do business with and says you are a victim of identity theft, contact the bank or company directly. Don't provide any confirming personal or financial data. A legitimate call from a bank or credit-card company checking on your purchases will normally ask you only to verify the details of a questionable purchase, not your personal financial data.

If you become a victim of identity theft, immediately notify the bank or credit-card companies to enable them to cancel and replace your cards with new account numbers. In addition, it is vital to immediately contact the three major credit-rating bureaus and request they place a "fraud alert" on your file. If a criminal attempted to obtain your financial information and you refused, it is still imperative that you inform the company involved in the attempted scam to enable their fraud department to take appropriate preventive action.

To learn more about identity theft, contact the Federal Trade Commission's ID Theft Clearinghouse by calling 877-438-4338 or going to its Web site, www.consumer.gov/idtheftidtheft/.

## PYRAMID SCHEMES

All pyramid schemes are illegal, and all of them depend on the victim's naiveté and greed. An essential feature of such schemes is the promise that profits will be generated primarily from recruiting new members rather than the sale of products or services.

In legitimate multilevel marketing companies, profits are generated from the sale of goods or services. In illegal pyramid schemes, while a product or service may be involved incidentally, the primary feature is the recruiting of new members, whose financial contributions ultimately go to those at the top of the pyramid.

Pyramid schemes encourage individuals to join a plan where they essentially deposit funds that are passed on to those who joined before them. They are promised that they, too, will receive funds from those whom they recruit into the plan. In the last few years a new version has appeared. The plan is described as a "gifting club," in which the latest recruits give contributions to current members with the understanding that people who are recruited later will provide new contributions. Here's an example: John and his friends attend a meeting where a promoter encourages them to join a pyramid plan by "gifting" $2,000 or more to the scheme, which will then be transmitted to members who have previously joined. After John donates the $2,000, he then recruits ten other members, each of whom donates $2,000 of their money. John eventually receives $20,000.

While this plan appears at first glance to be great, the only way it can continue and provide gains for new members is if an enormous number of new members join and contribute $2,000. This cannot go on forever, so every pyramid plan eventually runs out of new recruits and fails.

How should a Christian view the moral implications of a pyramid scheme? First, you should recognize that the government has outlawed such schemes. Second, Jesus Himself warned against the sin of allowing our greed to motivate us to obtain wealth from others: "Whatsoever ye would that men should do to you, do ye even so to them" (Matthew 7:12). In addition, we must avoid any business transaction that leads us to attempt to gain unethically from another person's actions. The apostle Paul declared, "Be not deceived; God is not mocked: for whatsoever a man soweth, that shall he also reap" (Galatians 6:7).

Even though you might profit financially from a pyramid scheme, your reputation will be damaged. Victims and their families will resent that they lost their precious savings so you could benefit. In the Bible we are told, "A good name is rather to be chosen than great riches" (Proverbs 22:1). When you consider that the nature of a pyramid scheme will inevitably result in the final recruits losing their money and possibly their faith, there is no question that you should steer clear of these schemes.

## Chain-Letter Schemes

Chain letters promise a phenomenal return for a small investment. A typical chain letter contains a list of a dozen people along with simple instructions. You are usually requested to send money ($100, for example) to the top person on the list. Then you are to remove the top person from the list, lifting the second person into the top position, and add your name to the bottom position. You are then to make a designated number of copies of the letter and mail them to your friends. The idea is that you will eventually receive $1,200 in return.

There are three problems with chain letters: They are illegal in most states if money is involved! They are immoral! And they won't work!

But these schemes are popular for two reasons: The first people on the list make serious money, which appeals to our sinful desire to get something for nothing. And most people cannot understand the geometrical progression needed for this scheme to continue to work. By the time your name comes to the top of the list, there would have to be tens of millions of people involved in the scheme for you to benefit.

Many people who receive chain letters remove all other names on the list and place their name first, followed by friends' names on the list they forward to other recipients, so you wouldn't receive any money. Most chain-letter schemes are forwarded through e-mails, often using headers like "Get Rich Quick," "Free University Degrees," "Free Vacation," or "Virus Alert." Stay away from e-mails with these kinds of titles on the subject line.

### Travel-Fraud Scams

Offers for vacations and so-called free airline trips are designed to lure innocent consumers into purchasing products or services. Such offers are fraudulent, because the offer is not free if it requires you to purchase a product or service to obtain the trip. Beware of replying to unsolicited e-mails for travel offers, even if you reply merely to request they remove your address from their list. Fraudulent or spam e-mail senders use such a response as confirmation that your e-mail address is valid, and they will continue to solicit your address and usually will sell your e-mail address to other spammers. Often the best approach is to delete the unwanted e-mail and indicate to your e-mail program (if possible) to refuse further messages from that source.

If you are tempted to accept an unsolicited offer for a "free" or unbelievably inexpensive vacation, then be alert to the possibility of hidden costs, charges, and taxes that may be revealed only after you accept the offer. Sometimes the free travel offer requires you to bring along a companion, who will be forced to pay the full fare. Carefully check the fine print. It is common for such offers of free trips to be restricted to undesirable dates or times. In addition, some people have found that the promised vacation spot is sold out and an alternative trip or vacation is substituted at a much higher price.

Offers of free vacations or prizes frequently involve your having to endure a two-hour high-pressure sales presentation that attempts to obligate you to immediately commit to purchase something. Be sure to do your own research through travel agencies and the Internet so you can compare the "free" offer with other attractive travel and vacation opportunities available from competitive travel companies.

One of the best ways to protect yourself is to always pay for such travel arrangements with a credit card. This will enable you to contest the charges if problems occur. Under U.S. law, your liability is limited to $50 if a company attempts to charge your credit card without your authorization.

### Charity Fraud

It is unfortunate, but our charitable instincts are also subject to attack by dishonest individuals. Of the hundreds of thousands of charities in our country, the vast majority are genuine and effective in their efforts to assist those in need. According to the 2004 annual report on charitable giving by the American Association of Fundraising Council's Trust for Philanthropy, philanthropy by individuals and corporations continues to rise each year. The report for 2003 indicates that Americans donated $240 billion, an increase of 2.8 percent from 2002.[3]

Unfortunately, criminals often take advantage of our desire to assist those in need. As a general rule, avoid donating money to any unfamiliar charity. Since there are thousands of legitimate charities, it makes little sense to give money to those who solicit your support out of the blue. If you are interested in supporting a previously unknown charity, first check it out with the Better Business Bureau. Check out any national charity at the BBB Wise Giving Alliance Web site, www.give.org, or call 703-276-0100. If you have any doubts about a request for a donation, do not hesitate to ask for information in writing. Any legitimate charity will be happy to supply ample written documentation of its history, aims, and financial results.

Many fraudulent charitable schemes attempt to deceive victims by using an organization name that is similar to a well-known charity. After a time of great tragedy, a large number of fake charities will arise, taking advantage of other people's suffering. For example, after the tsunami tragedy in the Indian Ocean in December 2004, fake charities immediately made phone calls and sent e-mail spam, preying on the generosity and compassion of well-meaning people. But rather than helping the hundreds of thousands of victims, they only helped criminals get richer. After disasters or other catastrophic events, limit your giving exclusively to well-known charities that you trust.

Part 3

# Protecting Your Family's Financial Goals

# Chapter 9

# Insuring Against Financial Disaster

*Choosing the Best Policies to Protect Your Assets*

*Airline insurance replaces the fear of death
with the comforting prospect of cash.*
—CECIL BEATON

N o one likes to think about how he would be affected financially if a family member died prematurely, became chronically ill, or lost significant work time due to a major injury. But to protect your family and your plans for financial independence, you need to think about all of these possibilities. The high cost of healthcare, the loss of income due to an inability to work, and the financial impact on a family due to the death of a wage earner—all can quickly destroy your hard work to achieve financial freedom.

Assuring that your family has adequate insurance coverage—health, life, homeowner's, auto, disability, and even long-term-care insurance—is an essential element in your planning for financial independence. You need to wisely use the tool of insurance to protect your financial goals against the crises of life.

The apostle Paul wrote about our responsibilities to provide for our family's security: "But if any provide not for his own, and specially for those of his own house, he hath denied the faith, and is worse than an infidel" (1 Timothy 5:8).

## ESTATE PLANNING

You spend a lifetime working hard, saving, and investing to create your estate, so it is certainly worth spending a few hours every year with a professional insurance and financial planner, plus your accountant, to protect these vital assets for you and your family. In preparing your estate plan, it is important to carefully consider your long-term financial goals.

For almost two decades I was a Chartered Life Underwriter (CLU) and a professional financial planner. During those years I interviewed thousands of individual, professional, and business clients. I would ask the following questions to clarify their financial strategies, their long-term goals, and their lifestyle concerns. Write down your answers to these questions as you prepare to meet with a professional estate planner or CLU. Use your responses to clarify your family's situation and its future needs.

> *When a man retires, his wife gets twice the husband but only half the income.*
> —*Chi Chi Rodriguez*

How do you feel about

- your financial obligation to provide a comfortable lifestyle for your family?
- your spouse's ability to handle your estate assets after you are no longer here to participate in decision making?
- your spouse making major family decisions in your absence?

- your family receiving a guaranteed annual income after your
  death—from your investments and insurance—to support their
  standard of living?
- the adequacy of your current retirement plans to meet your goal
  of a comfortable retirement for you and your spouse?
- the adequacy of your existing group insurance coverage, together
  with your personal life insurance and disability insurance, to protect your loved ones if you should be disabled or die prematurely?
- the percentage of your current standard of living that you would
  want to maintain for your spouse and children in the years following your death?

Discuss your answers with your spouse and with your professional estate
planner. Use your responses as well when you talk with the lawyer who will
prepare your wills and power of attorney. These answers should guide you
in the preparation and revision of your will and your spouse's will and also
in determining how much and what types of insurance you and your family require.

## LIFE INSURANCE

Most of us recognize the importance of insuring our homes and cars. However, many people fail to adequately insure their monthly income despite
the fact that this income supports everything else in their lives. Most financial experts agree that the principal wage earner should acquire life insurance coverage equal to eight to ten times his or her annual salary. The
tax-free death benefit paid by your life insurance can be invested to generate a guaranteed income to help preserve your family's standard of living
after your death. And since in many families both husband and wife generate significant income, it is essential to provide life-insurance protection
to cover the lost income of both spouses.

Find a qualified professional insurance broker or agent who can analyze your insurance needs and provide you with proper life insurance and disability insurance. Make certain the broker or agent can provide competitive quotes from a number of excellent insurance companies. It is unwise to deal with an agent who represents only one company, because that agent can offer only one insurance option.

Your ability to earn an income during your early and middle years is your greatest single financial asset. But one day the income from employment will end due to retirement, disability, or premature death. While a wise long-term investment program will eventually accumulate enough capital to provide a guaranteed retirement income, usually beginning at age sixty-five, a problem occurs if premature death cuts short your working years. In this case, wills and life insurance can provide financial security for your family.

Husbands who leave their widows and children without an adequate guaranteed income did not plan to fail to provide; they simply never got around to providing the income protection their family needed. Although some living expenses will naturally be reduced when the chief wage earner dies, most housing expenses and family living costs will not significantly decrease.

Use the following percentage guidelines to calculate the amount of annual income your family will need to maintain its present standard of living after your death:

| Annual Gross Income | Percentage of the Gross Income Required to Maintain Your Family's Standard of Living (assuming your debts and mortgage are paid off) |
|---|---|
| $24,001 to $32,000 | 70% + |
| More than $32,000 | 65% + |

In addition to providing a guaranteed income for your survivors, your life-insurance benefit should also be large enough to pay off all outstanding debts and mortgages. A debt should last no longer than the person who created it. Paying off your home mortgage and outstanding debts or business loans is one of the primary benefits you can provide with a life-insurance policy. Life insurance is a unique financial tool that provides the largest possible tax-free benefit at the moment the funds are most urgently required—at the death of the family's major income provider.

You might believe there is little need for life insurance if your spouse is young and you think she would likely soon find a new husband to support her and the children. However, statistics reveal that most widows, no matter what age, do not remarry. Between the ages of twenty-one and thirty, fewer than 25 percent of widows remarry. Less than 10 percent of widows between the ages of thirty and forty remarry after the death of their husbands.[1] If a widow has children, the odds against her remarriage are even higher. Therefore families need an adequate amount of life insurance to guarantee they can remain in their existing home and allow the children to retain their neighborhood, church, school, and friends during the difficult period following the loss of a parent.

### How Much Insurance Do You Need?
How can you determine the proper amount of life insurance? While you could use a number of sophisticated formulas, I have provided a simple questionnaire and formula at the end of this chapter to determine the amount of insurance you need.

### Take Out Insurance on Both Spouses
One area that many couples unwisely ignore is the need for adequate life insurance on the spouse who earns the lesser income. For instance, when a wife dies before her husband, it creates a significant financial hardship that

can destroy all the plans they shared for educating their children and providing for a comfortable retirement. If a wife works outside the home, her
income should be provided for through life insurance in the same manner
as her husband's. Even if a wife is a stay-at-home mom, you need life insurance to cover the considerable cost of day care, housekeeping, and other
things your family would need after her death.

Usually a couple's lifestyle and standard of living, including mortgage
payments and retirement plans, depend on the wife's continuing income
just as much as the husband's. The loss of her income could create a financial disaster. A solution to guaranteeing her income is a joint life-insurance
policy that will pay the same death benefit to the survivor, whichever
spouse dies first. A joint term-life-insurance policy can provide substantial
savings (10 percent or more) on your insurance premiums compared with
the cost of buying two separate policies.

### Preserve Your Estate from Death Taxes

Life insurance is also a useful financial tool for wealthy individuals whose
survivors will find that the government's demand for immediate payment of
death and estate taxes will drain the liquid assets even from a large estate.
In effect, Uncle Sam has a "mortgage" on everything that wealthy people
believe they own. Very often, large estates must be sold in a hurry at a deep
discount to provide the immediate cash needed to pay estate taxes, which are
due shortly after death. However, if people purchase adequate life insurance
to pay the taxes due at death, their estates will be preserved intact. If those
who are wealthy do not provide for paying estate taxes through adequate life
insurance, death taxes may wipe out a significant part of their estate.

### Take Advantage of Rate Discounts

While most Christians would qualify for lower life insurance rates available
to nonsmokers and nondrinkers, few people realize they can ask their insur-

ance companies to reevaluate and give them nonsmoker and nondrinker discounts on policies they bought years ago. These special discounts are often applicable to homeowner's and auto insurance policies as well.

In addition, you should always shop around for the best rates. Most insurance agents and brokers will be able to provide you with competitive quotes from dozens of companies for life, disability, fire, and automobile insurance so you can get the best terms, discounts, and premium rates. Always choose large, well-known companies. It is wise to check out the financial stability of the insurance companies you are interested in by looking at their financial ratings at A.M. Best or Standard & Poor's.

### Opt for Term Life Insurance

There are two main types of life insurance: permanent and term. Permanent insurance, including whole-life and universal-life policies, combines pure term life insurance protection with a savings element. Due to the low interest rate earned historically on permanent insurance policies, you should always buy pure term insurance and place your investment dollars with other companies, such as mutual funds. Term insurance provides life insurance protection for a predetermined number of years. Term insurance rates are inexpensive and extremely competitive among many insurance carriers, so you should ask your insurance broker or agent to shop around for the best rates. Insist on your broker or agent providing dozens of competitive quotes. Many companies will issue an insurance policy for $100,000 protection for a healthy thirty-five-year-old male nonsmoker for an annual premium of less than $180, or $15 per month.

These low rates make it possible for almost anyone to acquire adequate life insurance at an affordable cost. Renewable term-insurance policies are available for one, five, ten, or twenty years or for longer terms such as coverage until age seventy. Occasionally, someone who is age sixty or older may need to purchase a permanent insurance policy to acquire protection that will continue providing funds beyond age seventy to age one hundred. Wealthy individuals may need life insurance to last past age seventy to provide funds to pay estate and death taxes. Consider special term-insurance policies that will provide protection for ten or twenty years if you are age sixty-five plus and require protection for your estate for a shorter duration. Although expensive, these policies may be worthwhile for those who need protection against estate taxes.

## Maximize Your Group Insurance

If your employer offers group insurance, ask whether you can increase your life insurance coverage to a higher level than the standard amount of one or two times your annual salary. When you begin a job or have an annual performance review, you may be able to exercise an option to increase your coverage. It is worthwhile to obtain the maximum group insurance offered by your employer, because of the low premium rates and the less-stringent medical requirements. Make sure your named beneficiary on your group insurance and your company pension card is still correct. Unfortunately, it is common for people to forget to change the beneficiary designation of their group insurance or pension benefit following a divorce, a new marriage, or other significant change.

After their barn burned down, Julie called the insurance agent. "We had that barn insured for fifty thousand dollars," she said, "and we want our money."

"It doesn't work like that," the insurance agent said. "We will assess the value of the building and provide you with a new barn of comparable worth."

After a pause, Julie replied, "Then I'd like to cancel the life insurance policy on my husband."

## DISABILITY INSURANCE

Suffering a long-term disability is more likely than you think, but most people overlook the need to insure against it. If you lose significant work time due to an injury or illness, your plan for financial independence will be in jeopardy.

At age thirty-five, a person is *six times more likely* to suffer a long-term disability than to die before age sixty-five. A person between the ages of thirty-five and sixty-five has one chance in three that he or she will suffer a disability that will last longer than ninety days.[2] The real challenge is that the average length of such disabilities is at least five years. A disability of that duration would destroy almost anyone's plans for financial independence unless they had acquired an excellent disability-income insurance policy.

The odds are quite high that before you reach age sixty-five, you will suffer at least one disability that lasts three months or longer:

| CURRENT AGE | PROBABILITY OF DISABILITY |
|:-----------:|:-------------------------:|
| 25 | 44% |
| 30 | 42% |
| 35 | 41% |
| 40 | 39% |
| 45 | 36% |
| 50 | 33% |
| 55 | 27%[3] |

For most people, an uninsured long-term disability would quickly exhaust both their savings and their ability to borrow funds. Several studies reveal that the average American family would be financially exhausted if they missed only five monthly paychecks. Even if you saved 10 percent of your annual income for ten years to provide for a medical emergency, a long-term disability of only one year would wipe out your entire fund. The solution is to acquire a long-term-disability insurance policy, either through your employer's group insurance (if this is available) or by purchasing an individual disability policy through your insurance broker.

## HOMEOWNER'S INSURANCE

Homeowner's insurance protects you against financial loss occasioned by various insured perils such as fire, storm, and theft, as well as liability claims arising from a lawsuit. In the case of a lawsuit, the insurance company will pay the claim up to the amount of liability coverage and the legal costs to defend against the suit. In the case of a fire or damage from a storm or certain other causes, the homeowner's policy normally provides coverage on the contents of your home up to a certain percentage of the insured replacement value of the structure (often 40–50 percent).

### Cautions

Take note of several pitfalls that can imperil your coverage or inadvertently increase your premium. With the rise of fraudulent insurance claims and a higher number of legitimate claims in certain regions—due, for instance, to hurricanes, tornadoes, and other storm damage—and lower returns on corporate investments, many insurance companies have instituted procedures to avoid paying false or exaggerated claims. The first caution, therefore, is to pay claims yourself if they amount to only a few hundred dollars in excess of your policy's deductible. When you do this, do not inform your insurance company of your loss. If you report the loss even though you choose to pay for it yourself, you will likely lose your 10 percent claims-free discount. In addition, if you later make just one more claim, you may be identified as a high-risk client and will be forced to pay excessive future premiums or even be denied coverage. If your insurance company declines to insure your property, other insurance companies may also decline.

A second caution: when you complete an application for insurance, you must answer the required questions accurately. Any dishonesty or mistaken information on the initial application will result in a denial of your claim if your home is damaged and you file a claim.

A third caution: never call your insurance company directly to ask about possible coverage in the event of a future flood, hurricane, tornado, hailstorm, sewer-line backup, or other peril. Instead, read your policy terms carefully or talk to your agent (but *only* if he is an independent agent). If he or she works for the insurance company directly, then avoid asking such questions. The reason is simple. Many insurance companies will treat a simple client inquiry as a potential claim. This is true even if you do not file a formal claim. Then, under the two-claim rule, the next time you file an actual claim, the company will decline to renew your coverage on the basis that there have been two "claims" against that policy.

### Save Money on Homeowner's Insurance

Insurance premiums can vary widely depending on which company you choose. As you compare rates, always ask your agent or broker about available discounts. Consider the following suggestions to make certain you obtain the best coverage possible and minimize your premiums.

1. Shop around using the Internet and an established insurance broker who represents dozens of companies. To assure that you are obtaining the best quote available, complete your own research. Check companies on the Internet to compare coverage (go to NetQuote, www.netquote.com and Insurance Finder, www.insurancefinder.com). Also compare quotes and coverage with a reputable insurance broker who represents numerous high-quality companies. It is important to consider both service and price

when choosing the best carrier. Ask around to verify that the insurer you're about to choose has an excellent reputation for paying claims fairly and promptly.

Also, ask the agent or broker what options you have to reduce your premiums with discounts, such as nonsmoking, nondrinking, fire alarms, and low-claims history. In addition, examine the financial ratings of the insurance companies by inquiring with A.M. Best or Standard & Poor's rating services (listed in the appendix).

2. Ask your carrier to raise the amount of your deductible. The deductible is the amount of money you are responsible for paying to cover a claim before the insurance company steps in and pays the balance. Most policies have a standard deductible of $250. However, you can save on your premium by asking the company to increase the amount of your deductible. Insurance is designed to cover large and catastrophic claims that would otherwise become a threat to your financial well-being. You should pay smaller losses yourself.

### Estimated Savings from Increasing Your Deductible

The normal deductible is $250.
Increase deductible to $500: save up to 12 percent
Increase deductible to $1,000: save up to 24 percent
Increase deductible to $2,500: save up to 30 percent
Increase deductible to $5,000: save up to 37 percent
Your actual savings will depend on the rules and practices
    of each insurance company.

3. Consider buying both your home and car insurance from the same company. Many insurance companies grant a discount of up to 15 percent if you give them both your homeowner's and auto insurance business. Your

experience at the time of a claim is often better if the same company insures both your car and home.

4. Ask the insurance company to apply a discount if your home is relatively new or has high-quality construction materials. Some insurers will offer discounts of up to 15 percent if a house is new or has excellent-quality construction. Also, if your home is near a fire station or even a fire hydrant, ask your agent about an additional discount. When choosing a home, you can save on insurance premiums by avoiding an earthquake zone and a high-risk flood plain. Be aware that standard homeowner's policies do not cover damage from floods.

5. Limit coverage to the replacement value of the house and its contents. The land beneath your house has great value, but it is not subject to risk from fire, storms, or other insurable perils. Therefore, when you purchase insurance you should only pay for coverage equal to the full replacement value of the structure plus contents.

6. Consider improving your home's security features. Most insurance companies offer discounts of up to 5 percent if you protect your house with burglar alarms, deadbolt locks, and smoke detectors. Some companies offer discounts of up to 20 percent for clients who install advanced sprinkler firefighting systems or burglar warning systems that are monitored by and connected directly to the police and fire departments. It is a good idea to check with your prospective insurance company to determine the level of such discounts before installing a sprinkler system or a new security system.

7. Stop smoking and save. Every year in the United States more than twenty-three thousand fires are caused by smoking. Ask if your prospective insurer offers discounts to nonsmokers.

8. If you are a senior, ask for a discount. Some insurance companies offer anyone who is retired or older than fifty-five a premium discount of up to 10 percent, theorizing that stay-at-home residents are more likely to carefully maintain their home and be able to call in an alarm immediately.

9. Consider applying for group home-insurance coverage. If you belong to a business association or an alumni group, you might qualify for lower-cost home insurance that is available to members of your organization.

10. Ask for a discount for remaining a long-term client. Some insurance companies offer a 5–10 percent discount for clients who remain policyholders for five years or longer.

11. Conduct an annual review of your homeowner's policy. You should compare your insurance policy's levels of coverage with the actual value of your home and contents to make certain that all of your property is adequately covered. Conversely, if you have sold or given away significant belongings, there is no point in paying insurance premiums for excessive coverage.[4]

12. Make certain that your policy provides adequate liability coverage to protect your family from lawsuits. While the probability of a lawsuit is low, the risk is one that should be covered to protect your financial freedom. Liability coverage from $1 million to $2 million is essential.

## LONG-TERM-CARE INSURANCE

This type of insurance is increasingly vital for Americans who seek to protect themselves and their parents from the astronomical costs of long-term nursing-home care. Current estimates indicate that the cost of nursing-home care ranges between $40,000 and $100,000 annually. High-end nursing homes can cost $100,000 or more annually. Thus you must plan for this potential expense.

We all have to consider the threat to our financial goals posed by the potential cost of nursing homes and in-home medical care. Such care is likely to be needed by anyone who suffers from degenerative conditions (such as strokes), prolonged diseases (various cancers), or mental disorders (Alzheimer's, for example).

Up to seven million Americans will need long-term nursing-home care this year, and up to 40 percent of Americans over the age of sixty-five will enter a nursing home before they die. The enormous costs associated with such care can destroy even the best plans for financial independence unless you take advantage of available insurance tools, such as long-term-care insurance (LTC). Of all the insurance plans that might make a huge difference to your financial future, LTC is one of the most important. As a policyholder, you pay an affordable annual premium in the years prior to old age and before any age-related health crisis to enable the insurance company to step in and cover the insurable risk when you or your spouse might need nursing-home care.

Fortunately many employers offer cost-effective group insurance plans that include long-term-care insurance under a shared-cost formula. Since 1997 the IRS has allowed companies to deduct the cost of these premiums. If group long-term-care insurance is available to you, take advantage of it. If your employer does not offer a group LTC plan, research available private insurance coverage to protect your family's assets. The Internet and a well-established insurance broker are essential to find the best coverage at a competitive rate. Before purchasing an LTC policy, check the insurance company's ratings. (For a list of rating companies, see the appendix.)

If you are wondering if you actually need long-term-care insurance, consider the following:

- Nursing-home care can run as high as $100,000 annually, depending on the area, the level of service, and the quality of the care and facilities. For most people this cost will be far more than they can afford without ruining their financial plan.
- The average length of stay in a nursing home is approximately 2.9 years. However, people with Alzheimer's or some similar cognitive disease will average eight years. Such a long period of nursing-home costs will bankrupt most people.

- Many standard LTC policies offer a benefit that begins at day one and offers a $130 daily benefit that is protected against inflation. This benefit is guaranteed for up to six years of care. One California policy offered such long-term coverage for a healthy fifty-nine-year-old for an annual premium of $2,600. Obviously, premiums will vary from company to company. It is essential that you research and verify the financial stability of any insurance company that you entrust to protect you and your spouse (or your parents). At age sixty-five, the same type of coverage would cost approximately $3,800 annually, even if you are in good health. Despite the relatively high premiums, if you or your spouse ever needs nursing-home care, the cost of one year of care will quickly exceed the amount you have paid in premiums.
- Experience reveals that 50 percent of those who buy LTC insurance eventually use the coverage. This is remarkable when you realize that the vast majority of people who pay to insure a home and an automobile never actually benefit from a claim. You could argue that good LTC insurance is the best insurance bargain you will ever find.
- Many have not seriously considered their need for long-term-care insurance under the mistaken impression that Medicare will provide the needed coverage. However, Medicare rules are so restrictive that a study done in 2000 indicated that only 8 percent of those living in nursing homes were in a skilled nursing home and qualified for Medicare support, and then only if they were destitute.[5] Ninety-two percent of the people in this study were living in what are called custodial-care homes, thereby not qualifying for Medicare assistance. Medicare is not a realistic answer for a family's future nursing-home costs.

## HEALTH INSURANCE

Numerous studies reveal that the number-one cause of bankruptcy in the United States is the astronomical cost of healthcare following a medical crisis. In the span of only a few weeks, the costs of medical care will usually create such enormous bills that they will quickly wipe out the savings and retirement assets of most families. Unless a family has purchased adequate health insurance, it will often face financial meltdown. This area of insurance has so many provisions and complexities that you should meet with a professional health-insurance consultant to obtain the right coverage.

## CAR INSURANCE

It is vital that you research on the Internet and contact various insurance brokers to determine the best auto-insurance policies and lowest premiums available. To obtain the best policy, consider these suggestions:

1. Always shop around. You can access the most competitive insurance quotes by calling brokers or by visiting online quotation services. Once you submit your information to the insurance quotation Web sites, you will normally receive a competitive quote by e-mail within approximately an hour. Auto insurance quotation services include InsWeb (www.insweb.com), Nationwide Insurance (http://nwinsurance.nationwide.com/nwinsurance/), and for Canadian quotes, Kanetix (www.kanetix.com). The service manager at your car dealership should be able to offer advice about the fairness and timeliness of claims with various insurance companies he's worked with.

2. Consider buying an automobile that costs less to insure. Sports cars and high-priced luxury cars have the highest insurance premiums. Unfortunately, drivers of sports cars tend to have more accidents, and sports cars are usually much more expensive to repair. Some types of cars are much

more likely to be stolen and thus attract a higher insurance premium. SUVs and cars with sophisticated audio systems are also likely to attract a much higher insurance premium.

3. Ask if high-level safety and security features will save you money. In addition to possible discounts for added safety features, the larger your vehicle is, the less likely there will be severe passenger injuries in an accident. Ask your insurance broker about a discount if you drive a larger vehicle or if your vehicle has added safety and/or security features.

4. If you drive fewer miles, ask if you qualify for a discount. Some insurance companies offer discounts for drivers who lease their automobiles because the terms of the lease limit the mileage a driver can accumulate before incurring excess mileage charges.

5. Sign on with the American Automobile Association or the Canadian Automobile Association. These organizations provide excellent emergency roadside service, which is a major benefit. In addition, if you call them for service needed as the result of a minor accident, they guarantee they will not file an accident report with your insurance carrier. This is important because reporting minor accidents (even if you do not file a claim) can increase the cost of your future insurance premiums.

6. Check on savings for consolidating multiple policies with one company. Many insurance companies offer their best discounts to clients who insure all of their cars (and their home) with one insurer.

7. Carefully check on the insurance coverage provided by some credit cards for rental cars. Some cards, such as Visa, guarantee that the same deductible coverage on your collision and comprehensive protection on your auto policy will be extended to you while using a rental car paid for with that credit card. If you have that coverage, there is no need to pay for the expensive additional insurance coverage offered by car rental companies.

8. Add rental-car-fee coverage. If your policy does not cover the cost of a rental car while your vehicle is being repaired after an accident, add that

### Odd Insurance Claims

When I worked in the auto, fire, and commercial insurance field—as well as the life insurance and annuity field—I often heard about insurance claims that were bogus and others that were merely humorous. Here are some of the more interesting insurance claims that have been filed in recent years.

Question (by police officer): "Could either driver have done anything to avoid the accident?"
Answer (by one of the drivers): "Traveled by bus?"

Driver: "I collided with a stationary truck coming the other way."

Driver: "The pedestrian ran for the pavement, but I got him."[6]

coverage to your policy. Otherwise, you will pay the full cost of the car rental, possibly for weeks.

9. If you drive older vehicles, consider eliminating collision and comprehensive coverage. If your vehicle is worth less than $1,500, you'll probably come out ahead financially if you drop the nonessential coverage for such things as hail and wind damage (comprehensive) and damage caused by your own actions (such as backing your car into a tree). However, you must retain liability coverage.

10. If you drive a newer vehicle, ask for a higher deductible. If your car is worth more than $2,500, you can save money on collision and comprehensive coverage by increasing the deductible. Doing this might lower

your premium by as much as 25 percent. A safe driver shouldn't pay an unnecessarily high premium for a low deductible that might come into play only once in a decade. Remember: if the other driver is at fault, his insurance company will pay the claim (unless you live in a no-fault state).

11. Take a defensive-driving course. Some insurance companies grant a discount to drivers who take a defensive-driving course. Completing such a course could reduce the chances of your being involved in a serious accident and, as a result, reduces your insurance risk. If you are younger than twenty-five or have been involved in a previous accident, taking a defensive-driving course could save you money on premiums.

12. Check the "gap insurance" coverage on leased vehicles. If you lease your vehicle, make certain the terms of the lease include gap insurance that will reimburse you for the difference between your remaining lease obligation and the lower cash value of your leased vehicle if it should be stolen or destroyed in an accident.

## How Much Life Insurance Do I Need?

1. How much money will my family need to pay my debts, mortgage, and funeral costs? $ _____ (A)

2. What is my current annual income? $ _____ (B)

3. What percentage of my annual income do I want my family to receive? _____ %

4. The annual income amount that will be needed: _____ % x _____ (B) = $ _____ (C)

**Calculation**

How much insurance is needed to provide investment returns equal to C? Assume your family will invest the insurance proceeds at 5 percent net return after tax.

1. At 5 percent interest return, multiply the needed income _____ (C) x 20 = $ _____ (D).

2. Take the amount needed to pay all debts and mortgages upon your death _____ (A) and add it to the amount needed to provide a guaranteed income for your family _____ (D). A + D equals the total amount of insurance that is needed: $ _____ (E)

3. Add together the group and personal life insurance you already have: $ _____ (F)

4. Subtract the combined amount of your existing insurance _____ (F) from the total insurance needed _____ (E). E - F equals $_____. This last figure is the amount of additional insurance needed to meet your family's needs.

# Chapter 10

# The Necessity of Having a Will

*Preserving Your Estate for Your Family*

*Where there's a will, there's a lawyer.*
—UNKNOWN

U p to 70 percent of Americans die without having an enforceable will. This can produce a legal nightmare for the heirs, and it creates unnecessary delays in the distribution of assets. An up-to-date will is an essential part of your Christian stewardship. If you die without a will, you are giving strangers the right to determine how your estate will be handled. Without a will, you leave the distribution of your estate to the courts and laws of your state.

## WHY YOU NEED A WILL

At the time of your death, a will legally transfers your property to individuals and/or organizations that you have designated as your beneficiaries. A will is revocable (subject to change at your decision) until the time of your death. As a testamentary declaration, your will becomes legally effective only at the time of your death.

Unfortunately, many people suffer from an irrational fear that their decision to make preparations for a will may actually lead to an early death. Although such a fear is illogical, it is far from uncommon. This unspoken fear has led millions of otherwise practical people to avoid the essential duty of preparing their wills.

The goal of a carefully prepared and properly crafted will is to distribute your property at your death to whomever you wish. You are the one who determines how your estate will provide significant assets to your relatives and friends and to any organizations you choose. Your will instructs your executor to distribute your assets—such as monetary assets, a vacation cottage, a fishing boat, golf clubs, a coin collection, other real property, and a variety of personal possessions—to the appropriate beneficiaries.

A will also provides for your assets to be managed by your executor and provides for the care of your minor children by naming guardians for them. One of the most important purposes of a will is to direct a court to appoint someone you trust as the legal guardian of your minor children. While the court will officially designate the guardian, your will has a powerful influence on the court's decision. It is essential that you provide financial resources from your estate so the guardian can care for your children.

If you are the primary breadwinner, one of the major requirements of an estate plan is to provide an adequate ongoing guaranteed income for your family to replace your salary. Most people who die prematurely will not have been able to accumulate sufficient investment funds prior to death to pay all outstanding debts plus any estate taxes due and also provide a guaranteed income for their family for a significant number of years. The solution is to use the tools of a well-written will, excellent investments, and adequate amounts of life insurance that will produce a guaranteed monthly income during the years that your family will need this income support.

### To Care for Your Minor Children

When you have children, you have a moral responsibility to provide for them financially, even after your death. You do this by appointing a legal guardian who will care for them if you are not available. If you fail to appoint a guardian, you surrender this incredibly important duty to a stranger appointed by a court, who will make the vital decisions regarding your children and their future without any direction from you.

The selection of a legal guardian should be carefully considered and discussed with the prospective guardians. Ideally you will find another couple who shares your religious and lifestyle views. It is not essential that the guardians have children of their own, but most parents choose people who have experience raising children. After you have come to an agreement, you then nominate them in your will as legal guardians in the unlikely event of the premature death of both you and your spouse. Many couples choose a crisscross arrangement of guardianship. In a crisscross arrangement, each set of parents agrees to care for the others' children in the case of the couple's death.

### To Distribute Your Assets

Even if you are single, you need to prepare a will to avoid your estate being distributed according to the inflexible rules established by state law. The only way you can take control of the distribution of your assets is to prepare a legal will.

Every state has its own laws regarding the final distribution of property for those who die without a legal will in effect. In addition, each state has laws that determine what constitutes a legally valid will. Despite the easily accessible forms in stores and on the Internet that help you write a will, I strongly encourage you to engage the services of a lawyer to complete your will for yourself and your spouse. Any mistake in the form—the wording, the witnessing, or the signing—can result in your will being declared invalid. If this occurs, then you fall into the same situation as those who have no will at all. It is unwise in the extreme to spend a lifetime working hard and investing to build an estate for you and your family and then (to save a few hundred dollars of lawyer's fees) make common mistakes in your store-bought will that will create untold financial and legal problems for your beneficiaries.

If you die intestate (without a legally valid will), the state courts will distribute your assets among your next of kin according to a rigid legal formula that does not take into consideration your desires or the special needs of your family members. If you do not have an immediate family and you choose to die without a legally valid will, the government will seize your property in a procedure appropriately called "escheats."

## PLANNING AND WRITING YOUR WILL

Virtually everyone who is married, single, divorced, or widowed needs a will. If you have dependents and loved ones you care for, you need a carefully planned will. In today's legal climate each spouse needs a separate will to provide for the proper distribution of the estate following his or her death.

Both husband and wife should be familiar with all their insurance policies, the location of all bank and trust accounts and legal documents, as well as the contents of safety-deposit boxes. Nothing is more tragic than a widow living in poverty while cash, stocks, and bonds of her deceased husband lie undiscovered in an unknown bank, trust company, or safety-deposit box.

Before you meet with a lawyer, carefully answer the questions in the will-planning questionnaire found at the end of this chapter. Your attorney will find it much easier to give advice after you and your spouse have assessed the key issues regarding your estate. The two of you should fill out the questionnaire separately (make an extra copy) to help your lawyer prepare a set of wills that will protect your family and provide for the wise distribution of your estate. In addition, your attorney can advise you on how you can minimize taxes that might otherwise decrease your estate. Make it an immediate priority to meet with a lawyer to complete your wills after you carefully complete the questionnaire.

Revise and update your will whenever you have a significant change in your life or family situation, such as the birth of another child, a marriage, a divorce, a bankruptcy, acquisition or sale of a business, or whenever a significant change in the tax laws will impact your estate distribution. Also, if a beneficiary or an executor dies or leaves the country, you should update your will.

By law, a new marriage invalidates an existing will, and therefore you are required to prepare a new will. If you fail to draft a new will following your marriage, your earlier will is considered invalid by the courts.

If there are no major changes to your life situation, you don't need to change your will. Even if it is decades old, it remains valid. If you move from one state to another, ask a lawyer if you should update your will, even if children have not been added to your family. However, in this day of continuing changes in taxation, it is prudent to review your will with a competent attorney every five to ten years.

> *When an elderly woman met with her pastor to talk about the funeral service she wanted, she had two requests. First, she wanted to be cremated, and second, she wanted her ashes scattered over Bloomingdale's. "Why Bloomingdale's?" the pastor asked.*
> *"That way I know my daughters will visit me twice a week."*

## JOINT OWNERSHIP

Joint ownership of property can be used to transfer property upon a person's death. The beneficiary's name is added to the title of the property, making the two people joint owners. This method works well for couples who have a long-term, trusting relationship. It allows a home or bank account to be transferred immediately with legal probate from a deceased spouse to the survivor. However, while this is a popular option, there are many dangers to this method of estate planning.

I strongly advise against joint ownership of property, except for joint homeownership and joint bank accounts for husbands and wives with a long-term, trusting relationship. Joint ownership can be an enormous problem when people use this method to transfer property to someone other than their spouse. While it is easy to add someone's name to a title on a property, if you later change your mind, you cannot remove the person's name without his or her written permission or a court order.

If you add your son's or daughter's name to the title on your home in anticipation of transferring it at your death, you may face financial disaster if your child subsequently falls into deep debt or divorces a spouse. Your child's creditors could force the sale of your home, or the divorced spouse might demand his or her share of your home as "joint marital property." Your co-owner might transfer his or her half of the title to someone else without your approval or without your knowledge. If you choose to add a minor child as a joint owner, you will be unable to sell or refinance the property without a court granting approval, since a minor cannot legally sign on his or her own behalf.

In light of numerous horror stories where parents have lost their property through the unwise use of joint ownership, I strongly advise you to use a will to transfer your properties to your beneficiaries upon your death. An alternative is to use a living trust to protect yourself.

## A LIVING TRUST

Living trusts are legally known as "inter vivos revocable trusts." "Inter vivos" means that the living trust takes effect while you are still alive, unlike a "testamentary trust," such as a will, which only takes effect at your death. The term "revocable" simply means that as long as you are alive, you retain total control to change or cancel the living trust. In the United States a living trust will allow you to control and protect your estate, maintain total privacy, and avoid probate costs and lengthy delays after your death. Your living trust becomes the legal owner of the assets that you transfer to the trust, and it continues to live on legally after your death.

In contrast, if you use a will, the courts can take as long as two years to probate the will. In addition, probating a will can produce executor and probate costs equal to as much as 10 percent of your estate. Probate also makes your financial affairs public documents, exposing financial details to other people.

When you discuss the options with your lawyer, he or she will advise you of the best way to protect your estate from taxes. Your lawyer will also include the proper clauses to allow the transfer of your estate to your beneficiaries following your death. If you choose to set up a living trust, you will become the grantor or settler and will remain the only one who can make changes to your trust. You can choose to be the sole trustee of your trust, or you can make your spouse your co-trustee. If you die or become incapacitated, your trustee will continue to control your estate without involving the probate court. Some individuals choose to appoint a professional corporate trustee, such as a trust company. Regardless of who is appointed, as long as you are medically competent, you can change the trustee at any time. In your living trust document, you should name a trusted individual, such as a child or other relative, to act as the successor trustee to protect your interests in the event you become incapacitated.

When you die, the successor trustee will act in the same manner as an executor for a will, except that your estate will escape the costs, publicity, and the legal delays of reporting to a probate court. You can name individuals or organizations as the beneficiaries in your living trust to receive the proceeds of your estate when you die. If you should become incapacitated by disease or accident, your successor trustee will step in to administer your estate for your benefit as long as required. However, because you have a living trust, there will be no court-appointed administrator. As a successor trustee, this person has a legal fiduciary responsibility to act responsibly in your financial best interest, including the payment of any estate taxes that are due.

> *One man's last will and testament stated, "Being of sound mind, I spent it all."*

## Avoid Common Mistakes

If you decide to prepare your own will using forms from the Internet or an office supply store (despite my strong urging that you use a lawyer), you should carefully review the following list of common mistakes. These mistakes may cause major problems or even invalidate your will. To make certain your will is legally valid before the probate courts, carefully review this information.

1. In most states you must sign your will in the presence of two witnesses who are *not* beneficiaries of your will. The witnesses must affirm that they saw you sign the will and also observed the other witness signing it as well. The probate court will eliminate any beneficiary to a will if he or she signed as a witness.

2. If you choose to use a store-bought will or one you downloaded from the Internet, make certain that its language conforms to the laws of your state.

3. Never attempt to totally eliminate your spouse as a beneficiary due to continuing marital discord. Regardless of whether you still love your spouse, under state law you must provide your spouse a certain minimum amount of your estate. If you do not do this, your spouse can challenge your will in court following your death.

4. When appointing your children as beneficiaries, it is dangerous to name them specifically. For example, if you name your three children and then later have a fourth child and neglect to update your will to include that child, when you die, you will have unintentionally disinherited that child.

5. Find out whether your state has separate property laws or community property laws. If you live in a separate-property state (the majority of states), then the assets and income you and your spouse acquire during your marriage will belong to each of you separately and will be subject to your personal desires as to their distribution at your death. If you live in a community-property state (Arizona, California, Idaho, Louisiana, Nevada, New Mexico, Texas, Washington, or Wisconsin), each spouse is legally entitled to 50 percent of the assets acquired during your marriage. This includes the income each spouse earns, regardless of who purchased the assets or earned the money. Therefore, in your will you can only give away your share of the community property and any separate property you may own.

6. Avoid a joint will. When you have a joint will and your spouse dies, it is very difficult to make changes in the document. A joint will can also result in the assets of your marriage being tied up until your death. A separate will for each spouse will avoid these complications.

7. One of the reasons to use a lawyer is to avoid language in your will that is legally ambiguous and can lead to confusion and possible conflict between unhappy beneficiaries. Unclear language can open the door to lengthy legal disputes that do not serve your family's interests. If the language of your will is confusing, the probate court may change your will to respond to a relative's legal challenge.

8. There are certain kinds of property that need to be distributed at death outside your will. Some of these assets include joint bank accounts, jointly owned real estate, or assets such as life-insurance policies and pensions that have named beneficiaries. In addition, assets that you have previously transferred to a living trust will not be subject to your will.

> *Relatives came from long distances to hear the reading of the will. The lawyer opened the document and began: "To my cousin Ed, I leave my ranch. To my brother Jim, I leave my money-market accounts. And to my cousin George, who always sat around and never did anything but wanted to be remembered in my will, I say, 'Hi, George.'"*

9. Anyone who owns property in another state must write a separate will following the rules of that state for out-of-state property ownership.

10. Your executor must understand your wishes and be competent to carry out those wishes following your death. Choose an executor who is wise, responsible, and trustworthy to carry out the terms of your will.

11. Any revisions to your will must follow the rules of your state. If they do not, a probate court may reject those changes. When you change your will, obtain all copies of the old will and destroy them to eliminate possible confusion. Make certain that your lawyer, your executor, and your major beneficiaries all have a copy of your latest will.

12. Even if you decide to write your own will, have a lawyer who is familiar with estate planning review your document to make certain there are no mistakes that could cause problems. The small fee for such a service is well worth the peace of mind that your desires for your beneficiaries will be fulfilled. There is no point in spending a lifetime building your estate and then taking a chance that it will not fully benefit those you love.

## WILL-PLANNING QUESTIONNAIRE

Your answers to these questions will assist your lawyer in completing your will and advising you in estate planning. Both spouses should fill out the questionnaire separately (make an extra copy) to help you assess the key issues regarding your estate.

1. Husband's name (first, middle, last): _____
   Soc. Sec. no.: _____
   Date of birth: _____

2. Wife's name (first, middle, last): _____
   Soc. Sec. no.: _____
   Date of birth: _____

3. Primary home address:

   _____

4. Secondary real-estate address:

   _____

5. Mailing address (if different from above):

   _____

6. Home phone: _____
   Husband's work phone: _____
   Wife's work phone: _____

7. Do you own other real estate? (include addresses)

   _____

## Value of Real Estate

| Item | Market Value | Mortgage Outstanding |
| --- | --- | --- |
| Primary residence: | _____ | _____ |
| Second home: | _____ | _____ |
| Cottage: | _____ | _____ |
| Total value: | _____ | _____ |

8. Other Property (autos, boats, collections)     Value

| | |
| --- | --- |
| _____ | _____ |
| _____ | _____ |
| _____ | _____ |
| _____ | _____ |

9. Bank Accounts                    Estimated Account Totals

| | |
| --- | --- |
| _____ | _____ |
| _____ | _____ |
| _____ | _____ |
| _____ | _____ |

10. Trust Companies     Estimated Account Totals     Contact Person

| | | |
| --- | --- | --- |
| _____ | _____ | _____ |
| _____ | _____ | _____ |
| _____ | _____ | _____ |

11. Mutual Funds     Estimated Account Totals     Contact Person

| | | |
| --- | --- | --- |
| _____ | _____ | _____ |
| _____ | _____ | _____ |
| _____ | _____ | _____ |
| _____ | _____ | _____ |

12. Individual Shares    Estimated Account Totals    Contact Person

_____    _____    _____

_____    _____    _____

_____    _____    _____

_____    _____    _____

13. Life Insurance Policies (cash value, universal, annuity)

Life Insurance Co.    Cash Value    Contact Person

_____    _____    _____

_____    _____    _____

_____    _____    _____

_____    _____    _____

14. Lawyer's name, address, phone:

_____

_____

_____

15. Tax accountant's name, address, phone:

_____

_____

_____

16. Location of the latest wills and powers of attorney documents:

_____

17. Do you have a safe and/or a safety-deposit box?

[ ] Yes

[ ] No

(Do not write down the locations; however, you should let your spouse and lawyer know the locations.)

18. Are there any special instructions regarding your funeral arrangements?

_____

_____

19. Full names of children:

_____

_____

20. Is it possible that other children may be born to you before you next amend your will?

[ ] Yes

[ ] No

If you anticipate having additional children, you should not mention your existing children by name lest you inadvertently disinherit any future children. In most situations, your will should state that bequests to your children should be divided equally among all of your surviving children.

21. Whom do you wish to appoint as your executor and trustee to administer your estate? Most people nominate their spouse as executor if the marriage is strong. The lawyer who drafts the will is usually an appropriate person to assist your spouse as co-executor. Trust companies also provide strong assistance to an executor, and any fees can be charged to the expenses of the estate.

Name of executor and trustee:

_____

22. How do you wish to dispose of your home? Should it be given to your spouse absolutely? to your spouse for life with or without the power to sell or exchange? to your child or children equally? Or should the home be sold and the proceeds added to the residue of your estate?

_____

23. How do you wish to dispose of your household goods, personal effects, automobile, and other possessions? Should they be given to specified beneficiaries? Or should these assets be sold and the proceeds added to the residue of your estate to be distributed according to your will?

_____

24. Do you wish to leave any specific bequests to particular individuals, family members, charities, churches, or missions?
[ ] Yes
[ ] No
If you have faithfully tithed to your church and supported missions, consider providing continued support from your estate.

Name of church, mission agency or agencies, and other charitable organizations:

_____

25. Do you wish to make any special provisions in the event your spouse does not survive you for a period of thirty days?
[ ] Yes
[ ] No
For example, if your spouse dies within thirty days of your death, it is likely that he or she would not have had time to draft a new will reflecting his or her status as a widow or widower. Therefore, you would

be wise to include a clause that directs the distribution of your joint assets in the event that both of you die within a short period of time.

26. Do you have any particular instructions regarding your burial?

_____

If so, discuss them with your spouse and pastor so they know your wishes prior to the reading of the will.

27. Do you own any real estate outside the country?
    [ ] Yes
    [ ] No
    If so, what provisions do you want to make for the disposal or transfer of that property? You will need a separate will to deal with property that you own in a different country. There are often restrictions regarding the transfer of real estate in other nations that require special provisions that a lawyer can advise you to include in your will.

    _____

28. How do you wish to dispose of the residue of your estate after all debts, taxes, and special bequests are made?

    Method A. By outright gift or bequest to one or more persons (for example, to your wife and/or children).
    Method B. By providing a life income from your estate to one or more beneficiaries (such as your spouse) and then later distributing the capital or residue in a particular manner (for example, to your wife for her lifetime and then later to your grown children).

    _____

29. Whom do you wish to name as the guardian of your young children if both you and your spouse die while your children are minors? Ideally, you should find another like-minded couple who shares your Christian values and then mutually agree that you will act as guardians for each other's children in the unlikely event that both parents die prematurely. If you cannot find an appropriate couple with children, you should then consider a close friend or relative.

_____


30. You need to provide in your will for the expenses your guardian will incur in caring for and educating your children. Your will should specifically give the guardians full access to the necessary funds provided by your life-insurance policies if both you and your spouse die while your children are minors.

31. List the details of any other wishes, trusts, or provisions, such as charitable bequests or setting up of a trust fund to provide for the care and support of a minor niece or nephew or of a special-needs relative.

_____

# Chapter 11

# Powers of Attorney

*Essential Tools to Protect Your Family
and Your Property*

Most of us make some provisions for our death, but many people are unaware that they could lose control of their property and business in the event of an incapacitating injury, surgery, or illness. In many states a government trustee will seize control of your assets and business when you are temporarily incapacitated.

On average, you have a 40 percent chance of suffering an illness, injury, or disability before the age of sixty-five that will prevent you from working for three months or longer. And in many states, in the event of a debilitating accident or illness, a hospital or doctor is required by law to notify a government trustee that you are incapacitated. The trustee will step in to seize control of your business and estate. Your business can be destroyed in only a few months if your spouse or your business executives are unable to pay the bills because a government trustee interferes with or delays the way your business is conducted. To avoid such a crisis, set up an enduring power of attorney that appoints your spouse or some other trusted individual to act on your legal behalf.

## POWER OF ATTORNEY

A power of attorney is a legal document in which you appoint someone you trust completely with the legal and financial authority to make decisions regarding your finances and to act on your behalf if a disability prevents you from acting for yourself. The person to whom the power of attorney is given is an "attorney-in-fact," also called your "agent," "donee," or "attorney." However, this person does not have to be a lawyer.

You (the principal donor) can revoke an enduring power of attorney at any time and for any reason. If you ever feel uncomfortable with your existing choice, you can name a new agent without notifying anyone else—including the person you previously named as agent. Most happily married people make their spouses their agents under this agreement with the understanding that their spouses are the ones who are most likely to understand their wishes and principles and will act in their best interests. Your choice of who will wield your power of attorney is one of the most important decisions you will make concerning your financial success. The choice of a loyal, mature, and businesslike agent to exercise your power of attorney will ensure that your personal wishes are carried out.

A power of attorney can be limited to a specific legal matter, such as the sale of property or a particular purchase, such as a business. It can also apply to a specific period of time. However, most power-of-attorney documents grant a broad legal authority to the agent without a specific time limit. The legal authority of a power of attorney ends automatically upon the death of either the principal or the agent.

> *We have been promised a safe arrival, but not a smooth voyage.*
> *—Henry Dubanville*

While standard power-of-attorney forms are available at office supply stores, you would be wise to have your lawyer prepare the document to avoid common errors such as those involving witness signing. When you prepare or renew your will, your lawyer can normally prepare a power-of-attorney document at the same time with little additional cost.

You should make multiple copies of your power of attorney and give one to the agent you appoint, retain one each for your records and your spouse's records, and give one copy, together with your will, to your lawyer to be kept on record.

## A POWER OF ATTORNEY FOR PERSONAL CARE

A growing concern in this age of medical miracles is that doctors will use sophisticated technologies to keep a person alive in a vegetative state or coma long after any real hope of a meaningful, conscious life has disappeared. I strongly recommend that you discuss with your spouse, family, and doctor your desires about whether you wish your hospital or doctor to engage in "heroic" medical procedures to maintain your life after all hope of a meaningful and independent life is lost. The recent tragedy of the Terri Schiavo case illustrates the terrible problems that can arise if we fail to make our medical desires known in writing to our doctors and fail to appoint a trusted friend or family member with our power of attorney for personal care.

You can appoint your spouse or some trusted friend with your power of attorney for personal care to make decisions regarding your medical care. This person is authorized to make the decision to "give or refuse to consent to treatment" to maintain your life. By creating this power of attorney for personal care, you can ensure that your desires will be carried out at a time when you are unable to communicate your wishes. You can choose to leave the medical-care decisions to your agent, or you may choose in the document to specify your instructions regarding the use of heroic medical resuscitation efforts. You may also include "do not resuscitate" orders to any hospital staff. You can only sign a power of attorney for personal care while you are of sound mind. If you should become mentally incapacitated before signing this document, the courts would deem your signature invalid.

Statistics reveal that, with CPR, young and middle-aged people can often recover fully from a heart attack, but a significant majority of older patients (age seventy-five and up) who are revived with CPR have impaired faculties. You should discuss with your spouse and personal physician whether you wish medical staff to use CPR or other measures to revive you if you suffer a life-threatening medical crisis. To avoid possible lawsuits, doctors and hospitals will usually refuse to remove life support from a patient unless they obtain the written consent of someone who has the power of attorney for personal care.

Make multiple copies of your power of attorney for personal care: one for the person you appoint as your agent, one for your records, another for your spouse, one for your family physician, and one copy to be kept on record with your lawyer. In addition to the document, it is vital that you have an open and frank discussion with your spouse and family so they will know exactly what your wishes are. When you enter a hospital with a serious medical condition, you or your spouse should provide the hospital's doctors with a copy of this document. You should give a copy to your family physician and also discuss this matter with him or her, making sure your wishes are understood and will be carried out.

Power-of-attorney-for-personal-care forms are normally available at office supply stores and at most hospital information centers. They are so simple that most people can easily prepare them on their own without the assistance of a lawyer. However, one area of concern is that of witness signing. Please remember to have both witnesses (neither of whom is related to the principal or agent) sign as witnesses to the principal's signature in the presence of the principal and each other.

## A LIVING WILL

Do not confuse a power of attorney for personal care with a living will. A living will is a nonbinding and nonlegal document that clearly lays out your last instructions to your family and executor regarding issues that must be dealt with immediately following your death. Remember that a will may not be discovered or read by your executor for many days after an unexpected death. However, a living will is a document that instructs your family and friends regarding immediate issues, such as your chosen funeral arrangements and detailed instructions as to who should receive personal items from your estate.

A living will can avoid confusion as to the deceased's wishes about the details of the burial, the choice of an appropriate funeral service, and so forth. Unfortunately, many families avoid frank discussions regarding these matters. However, as Christians, we should have no fear of death, and we should make our desires known regarding our funeral arrangements to avoid family confusion or conflict.

# Part 4

# SUCCESSFUL RETIREMENT PLANNING

# Chapter 12

---

# Plan *Now* for a Successful Retirement

*Making the Most of Insurance, Investments,*
*Annuities, and Pensions*

*A family held a birthday party for their wealthy grandfather to*
*celebrate his new retirement. The grandchildren gathered around*
*him and asked him to share his secrets of becoming wealthy. "Well,*
*children, it was 1932 during the bottom of the Great Depression,*
*and I lost everything. I was down to my last nickel. I invested that*
*nickel in a Macintosh apple. I spent the whole day polishing the*
*apple, and at the end of the day, I sold the apple for 10¢. The next*
*morning I invested the 10¢ in two apples. I spent the entire day*
*polishing them and sold them for 20¢. I continued this system for a*
*month, by the end of which I'd accumulated a fortune of $12.50.*
*Then my wife's father died and left us $3 million."*

Most North Americans want to retire with two things: good health and financial independence. Both goals involve a lifetime of preparation. However, statistics indicate that most people arrive at retirement without having accumulated the necessary assets to live in financial freedom.

## RETIREMENT FACTS

A survey conducted by the American Savings Education Council (ASEC) found that only 54 percent of American employees have completed a retirement-savings-need analysis. This is significant in light of the fact that those who complete a retirement calculation will accumulate a higher amount of retirement savings than those who fail to study their needs. You can calculate your own retirement needs using the retirement-planning worksheet at the end of this chapter. This will show you how well you are preparing for the years of retirement, when you won't be earning a salary.

The ASEC study noted that longer life expectancies will have a major impact on your retirement. Approximately 25 percent of American workers will not live long enough to retire at age sixty-five. However, the 75 percent of Americans who will reach age sixty-five are very likely to need retirement income for as much as two decades. The study also found that 40 percent of employees retire earlier than they had originally planned, usually due to medical problems or disability. This trend increases the need for workers to aggressively add to their investment savings to be certain their retirement income will be sufficient.

The study found that those who retire are concerned they may exhaust their retirement income fund by living too long. If a retiree withdraws a maximum of 3 percent of his funds annually, he will not exhaust his retirement fund before he dies. However, if he is forced to withdraw 4 or 5 percent of the funds annually, he is likely to outlive his retirement fund unless he has a very well-diversified and strong portfolio.[1]

The Social Security Administration reports that an astonishing 25 percent of citizens over age sixty-five are in such bad financial shape they are forced to continue to work. The total liquid assets of persons age sixty-five and older are approximately $4,000 per capita.[2] To *choose* to work after age sixty-five is wonderful. But to *have* to continue working is tragic.

While most people dream of retiring with a comfortable income to enjoy their final decades, the reality is that the vast majority do very little planning or investing to accomplish the goal of an adequate guaranteed income after they retire. Up to 93 percent of men who retire at age sixty-five admitted that they had failed to provide adequately for their retirement years because they never established a definite savings-and-investment plan. Despite forty to forty-five years of faithful "nine to five" labor, they failed to save and invest enough to provide a significant amount of guaranteed income to supplement their minimal Social Security income. Remarkably, 87 percent of people retire at a virtual poverty level due to their lack of financial planning. Up to $2 million in income passed through their families' hands during forty-five years (at an average income of $43,000 per year), but they managed to keep and invest very little of this amount to provide for future retirement income. A survey by Decima Research discovered that 41 percent of Canadian citizens hoped to retire by or before their sixtieth birthday. However, the survey found that more than half of that group had no idea how much they needed to accumulate in their investment portfolio to achieve their retirement objectives.[3]

An indication of the lack of practical planning and sustained action toward achieving a successful retirement is revealed in a survey of Canadians conducted by the polling firm Compass. The survey found that a surprising 11 percent of Canadians were "planning" on winning the lottery to achieve their retirement income needs.[4] Incredibly, they were relying on an unrealistic hope against incredible odds rather than planning ahead and investing significant funds to achieve a comfortable retirement income.

The Decima study revealed that a remarkable 75 percent of Canadians surveyed believed that the Canada Pension Plan would provide their primary or secondary source of retirement income.[5] Despite widely publicized concerns about the relatively low level of pension income that will be provided by the Canadian and U.S. Social Security systems, most citizens accept that their government pension plan will provide the necessary income to allow them to enjoy a comfortable retirement.

Financially unprepared people must adjust one of three critical elements in their retirement planning: (1) their planned amount of retirement income, (2) the amount of money they need to invest each year between now and their retirement date to enhance their investments to be certain they achieve their goal of financial independence during retirement, or (3) the age beyond sixty-five to which they must continue working in order to supply the necessary income.

A 1999 Retirement Confidence Survey found that most American workers believe they will have to work much longer than their parents did before they can comfortably retire. Nearly seven in ten (68 percent) of those surveyed indicated they expect to keep working after they officially "retire" at sixty-five. Amazingly, only 50 percent of all workers surveyed in this study have calculated how much they will need to save to provide for a comfortable life in retirement.[6] According to a study in 2000 by the U.S. General Accounting Office, "In 1998, 48% of retired persons reported that they had no company pension income of their own or from a spouse." This study reveals that almost half of Americans are retiring after a lifetime of employment with virtually no pension income to supplement their Social Security check.[7]

## YOU CAN'T RELY ON SOCIAL SECURITY

When the U.S. Congress and President Franklin Roosevelt created the Social Security system in 1935, they set the date of entitlement at age sixty-five. At that time the average life span for Americans was sixty-two years. The government obviously did not expect that most Americans would live long enough to receive Social Security benefits. But today in North America the average male who is alive at age sixty-five will most likely live to age eighty-one. The average female alive at age sixty-five will live to age eighty-five. However, for those who live to the age of eighty, their likelihood of living to age ninety is very strong. A man aged eighty has a 25 percent chance of living to age ninety, while a woman aged eighty has a better than 50 percent chance of living to age ninety.[8]

The financial implications of this unprecedented increase in life span after retirement has imperiled the health of the Social Security system. "[In] 1960, there were nearly 7 working age people for every person over 65. In 2000, that number dropped to 4.5. By 2030, the OECD [Organization for Economic Co-operation and Development] expects only 2.5 people to be working for every dependent elderly in the developed world."[9]

According to William Bonner and Addison Wiggin, authors of *Financial Reckoning Day*, financial disaster faces the average baby boomer who waits past age forty-six to confront his need to accumulate significant assets for retirement. By the time a person reaches his midforties, he has run out of time to easily build a comfortable retirement account to provide the income he would like to enjoy during retirement.

Bonner and Wiggin wrote:

Three little numbers at the end of the world:
   (1) Average age of American baby boomers on Jan. 1, 2002: 46.
   (2) Average amount in retirement plan: $50,000.
   (3) Number of years at 6% growth to reach comfortable retirement income: 63.[10]

At age forty-six, with only nineteen years left until retirement, the vast majority of Americans have run out of time to comfortably accumulate a level of investments that will allow them to enjoy a lifestyle during retirement similar to what they enjoy today. Many people have ignored their need to save regularly and to prudently invest to build a reliable retirement income in the vain belief that they can depend on the government's provision of a monthly pension from Social Security. However, as Bonner and Wiggin point out, there is one other key number that is just as significant as the first three numbers: "Amount of money in U.S. Social Security Trust Fund: 0."[11]

Despite the hundreds of billions of dollars that have been taken from American taxpayers since the creation of the Social Security system, the government has saved none of it. Instead, the government has spent these untold billions as if they were part of the general tax revenues. If a private pension or insurance company acted in this irresponsible way, the executives would be sent to prison for financial fraud.

The Social Security premiums paid annually by working citizens are used to pay the current costs of the pension payments made each year to retirees. There are no reserves, no investments building funds for future pension payments. Generations of politicians have created a financial disaster that will derail the retirement hopes of a whole generation that will reach age sixty-five in the years following 2020. As a result, aside from those who succeed in accumulating their own retirement funds, millions of Americans will be forced to continue working to provide an income.

In 2004 the U.S. Federal Reserve Chairman, Alan Greenspan, stated, "A doubling of the over-65 population by 2035 will substantially augment unified budget deficits and, accordingly, reduce federal saving unless actions are taken."[12] He noted that pressure on the Social Security and Medicare systems will grow at a staggering rate as the percentage of Americans age sixty-five and over will double by 2035. The aging of baby boomers (those born between 1946 and 1964) will place an unbearable strain on the financial resources of the government to support the benefits that have been promised under Social Security and Medicare. One of three unpleasant things must give way under this pressure: (1) the benefits must be reduced, (2) the age for receiving benefits must be delayed, or (3) working Americans must substantially increase the Social Security premiums they are paying. None of these options are politically attractive to either politicians or average citizens.

Greenspan noted that according to the Social Security Trustee 2004 report, "The Social Security tax receipts, equal to 12.4 percent of a worker's salary, won't cover the entire cost of outlays starting in 2018."[13] So we cannot depend on Social Security benefits to provide a significant portion of our retirement income in the decades following 2018. If you are between the ages of twenty and fifty, you would be wise to plan for your retirement assuming that Social Security will not likely provide significant pension income. However, if you are now in your fifties, you may be fortunate enough to receive Social Security benefits until your death.

## RETIREMENT PLANNING

Most people spend less than an hour every year planning for their retirement. However, if the Lord tarries, the average Christian will live for ten to twenty years after receiving his or her final paycheck. The only way you can ensure that you and your spouse will enjoy the financial rewards of a well-earned retirement is to begin planning today.

One of the biggest and best tax breaks available for the average taxpayer is the tax deductibility of the contributions we can make to government-approved retirement pension plans. In the United States these are called 401(k)s and individual retirement accounts (IRAs); in Canada these are called registered retirement savings plans (RRSPs). These tax-sheltered funds will accumulate at a significant rate using compound interest to produce a guaranteed income after you retire.

You will gain a significant tax advantage by making your annual tax-sheltered investment at the beginning of each year rather than waiting until the last day of the year. Over thirty years, the investor who makes an annual tax-sheltered deposit in January will accumulate almost 10 percent more money. To evaluate your retirement planning, complete the worksheet at the end of this chapter. As you plan, consider the following factors.

### The Impact of Inflation on Your Pension Income

According to a report issued by the Social Security Administration, the impact of even low levels of inflation over the next three decades will have a devastating impact on the purchasing power of your pension dollars.

### PURCHASING POWER OF $1,000 IN 2004 DECLINES THROUGH THE YEAR 2035

| YEAR | INFLATION RATE | | |
|------|------|------|------|
|      | 3% | 4% | 5% |
| 2005 | $971 | $962 | $952 |
| 2010 | $837 | $790 | $746 |
| 2015 | $722 | $650 | $585 |
| 2020 | $623 | $534 | $458 |
| 2025 | $538 | $439 | $359 |
| 2030 | $464 | $361 | $281 |
| 2035 | $400 | $296 | $220[14] |

Ever-increasing life expectancies mean that your retirement income must last many years longer than for previous generations. In addition, the impact of both taxation and inflation on your retirement income means that it's vital you invest significant income as early as possible and that you choose your investments wisely. As chapter 7 illustrated, there are a number of excellent investments that can help you achieve your retirement goals. Other sources of income are listed on the following pages. As you learn the advantages and disadvantages of different investments, you will gain confidence in your long-term investment strategy. Once you have educated yourself regarding both investment strategies and specific investments, you will be prepared to work with a professional financial planner and other investment professionals who can help you and your spouse achieve financial independence.

## Social Security Benefits

The Social Security Administration sends working Americans an annual statement that estimates the amount of monthly Social Security pension benefit you and your spouse can expect to receive in retirement. If you do not have an up-to-date statement, you can call the Social Security Administration at 800-772-1213 and request an estimate of your expected pension earnings by mail. Enter this estimated Social Security pension benefit on the retirement-planning worksheet at the end of this chapter to determine how much income you need to contribute from your own investments to reach your retirement income goal.

## Tax-Sheltered Retirement Savings Plans

Most successful American investors now pay more than 30 percent of their highest income dollars in taxes. Therefore, the use of a tax-sheltered plan such as an IRA, a Roth IRA, or an employer-sponsored 401(k) plan will provide a much higher after-tax return on your investment dollars.

Compare the investment experiences of two brothers. Bill invested $100,000 and let it grow for thirty years in a tax-sheltered investment at 10 percent interest. His brother Mike failed to use a tax shelter. Mike paid 30 percent in income taxes on the annual 10 percent interest growth on his $100,000 investment. At the end of thirty years, Bill will have accumulated a total of $2,008,550 in his tax-sheltered retirement fund compared to only $842,390 for Mike, who chose not to use a tax shelter. Although both brothers invested the same initial amount ($100,000) and earned the same rate of return (10 percent) over thirty years, the brother who took advantage of the tax shelter accumulated an additional $1,166,160 in retirement funds!

If Bill can continue to earn a 10 percent annual return on his investment funds after he retires at age sixty-five, this $1,166,160 in extra investment earnings will generate an additional income of $116,616 each year for the rest of his life. Although this $116,616 will now be taxable, it is likely to attract a tax of less than 25 percent in retirement. This means that Bill will still generate an additional after-tax income of $87,462 every year of his retirement. If he lives for twenty years after retiring (which is probable), then Bill's choice to utilize a tax-sheltered approach—such as a mutual fund held within an IRA, a Roth IRA, or a company-supported 401(k)—will produce an additional retirement after-tax income of $1,749,240 during his retirement.

On the other hand, Mike, who chose to invest his initial $100,000 for thirty years without using a tax shelter, will accumulate a fund of $842,390, which will produce a retirement pension of only $2,150 every month with the same 10 percent return. The brother who utilized the tax shelter to accumulate his retirement funds will have almost four times the monthly income throughout his retirement! This example illustrates two vital factors in successful financial planning—tax sheltering your investment and using the awesome power of compound interest over a number of years.

### The Guaranteed Life Annuity Policy

With people living significantly longer, how do they make certain they won't outlive their retirement income? The best solution for most investors is to purchase a guaranteed life annuity policy from a large, financially solid life-insurance company. Such an annuity will guarantee you and your spouse a monthly income that will continue as long as either of you is alive. The monthly amount paid by the insurance company is considered by the Internal Revenue Service to be a blend of mostly nontaxable principal and a smaller portion of taxable interest. This guarantees you a maximum after-tax monthly income for the rest of your life. This is often the best method to maximize your after-tax monthly pension income on a tax-protected basis while guaranteeing that the monthly checks will continue as long as you or your spouse lives. A joint life annuity will provide a guaranteed monthly income that you cannot outlive, and it eliminates the concern about constant investment decisions.

### Tax-Deferred Variable Annuities

Variable annuities are sold by life-insurance companies and provide the advantage of deferring tax until you retire and begin receiving income. They provide valuable death benefits and other guarantees. The death benefits will protect your beneficiaries if you happen to die before you begin to receive retirement income. The annuity death benefit provides your loved ones with the money you have invested in the annuity minus an adjustment for any previous withdrawals.

The benefits of deferring income taxes on your investment in an annuity are considerable. For example, if you invested $100,000 initially, and your money compounded at 8 percent annually over thirty years, it would accumulate $1,006,266 with your taxes deferred. If you choose to receive a lump-sum distribution, you will pay taxes of $299,068. Your net amount after tax will be $707,198, which is significantly more than the $478,931 you would have earned on a comparable taxable investment at 8 percent over the same thirty-year period (assuming a 33 percent income-tax rate).

If you choose to withdraw funds or take a distribution before age fifty-nine and a half, a 10 percent federal tax penalty may apply. Naturally, the actual tax rates might vary for different assets and taxpayers, depending on capital gains and qualified dividend income. This illustration is meant to point out the advantage of tax deferral in your investment strategy. The hypothetical returns just mentioned do not include withdrawal charges, mortality and expense risk charges, administrative fees, or other contract charges that would reduce your final amount.

## A Reverse Mortgage

Many people reach their retirement years and discover they have less income than they need. After taking their Social Security pension, company pension income, and income generated from other investments (such as IRAs), they may still have a significant shortfall. It is not uncommon for people to find that, after a lifetime of work and saving, they are "asset rich and cash poor." In other words, they have accumulated a considerable amount of equity in their home, but they have not provided enough savings and investments to produce income to make up the shortfall of pension income.

A possible solution is a reverse mortgage. The name "reverse mortgage" is apt because the stream of mortgage payments is reversed. Instead of your making monthly payments to a mortgage-lending institution, the reverse mortgage lender will pay the customer either a series of monthly payments or a lump sum. In many cases the customer will choose to create a line of credit with the reverse mortgage lender and access the funds only as needed.

This financial tool can provide the solution to generating significant additional monthly income for the rest of your life, with the repayment of the mortgage loan occurring only when the homeowner dies or sells the home. This can unlock the equity you have accumulated in your principal residence without the need for repayment until the sale of your house or the death of both you and your spouse. No repayment is required as long as you or your spouse maintains your home as your principal residence. At the death of the final spouse, the outstanding loan will become due and will be composed of the loan principal and the accrued interest. It is not necessary to sell the house if other funds are available from the estate to repay the outstanding mortgage loan.

The amount of the reverse mortgage loan that is available to you will generally depend on a number of factors, including your age, the value of your home, the size of your home equity, and prevailing mortgage interest rates. The proceeds of a reverse mortgage are tax free and will not adversely affect your benefits from Social Security or Medicare. In a typical reverse mortgage, a couple aged sixty-five with $500,000 equity in their home might borrow as much as 32 percent ($160,000) in a lump sum or receive a guaranteed tax-free monthly payment of approximately $927.

The most popular type of reverse mortgage is insured by the Federal Housing Administration. These insured reverse mortgages are called Home Equity Conversion Mortgages (HECM) and are available in all states. Reverse mortgages are available from many banks, mortgage companies, and other financial institutions in the United States and Canada. To qualify for a reverse mortgage, all current owners of the home must be age sixty-two or older and must live in the house as their principal residence. The house or condominium must be a single-family residence and at least one year old.

The American Association of Retired People (AARP) provides a useful Web site (www.rmaarp.com) that discusses reverse mortgages and allows you to calculate approximately how much money a reverse mortgage might generate based on your situation.

### 401(k) Retirement Plans

The government allows companies to set up a special tax-sheltered retirement plan for their employees, called a 401(k) retirement plan. The employee may contribute annually through payroll deduction into this plan up to $13,000 ($16,000 for employees older than age 50), and these funds will accumulate tax free until retirement. Many companies contribute matching deposits to their employees' 401(k) plans up to a certain percentage. Both the employees' and employer's contributions accumulate tax free. Usually the employees are given several investment options, such as various mutual funds, where they can direct their 401(k) plans to invest their funds.

To encourage employees to keep their money in the plan until retirement, the government requires a federal income tax penalty of 10 percent of whatever you take out of the plan prior to age fifty-nine and a half. However, there is a special exemption from the withdrawal penalty for those age fifty-five or older who leave their employment through early retirement, resignation, or a firing.

You must withdraw your 401(k) funds prior to age seventy and a half. When your funds are withdrawn to fund your retirement, they will be taxable. The fundamental advantages associated with 401(k) plans are the matching contributions made by your employer and the tax-free accumulation of assets.

### 403(b) Retirement Plans

People who are employed by nonprofit organizations, including universities, hospitals, and IRS-approved charities (such as churches and ministries), are eligible for 403(b) retirement plans, which are almost identical in features and benefits to 401(k) plans.

### Individual Retirement Accounts (IRAs)

An individual retirement account (IRA) is an IRS-approved tax shelter that you can establish separate from any employer's retirement plan. For example, in 2005 you can invest up to $4,000 for yourself and another $4,000 for your nonemployed spouse. You can deduct these contributions from your taxable earned income each year, and the investment account will accumulate tax free until you withdraw the funds in retirement. However, the funds that you withdraw in retirement will be fully taxable. As with a 401(k) plan, you cannot withdraw any funds before age fifty-nine and a half without incurring a 10 percent penalty.

Several situations allow you to withdraw funds from your traditional IRA without attracting the penalty: death, total disability, catastrophic medical expenses exceeding 7.5 percent of your adjusted gross income, your first purchase of a house (maximum withdrawal of $10,000), or education costs for any immediate family member for secondary, graduate, or postgraduate school.

> *Retirement is like a long vacation in Las Vegas. The goal is to enjoy it to the fullest, but not so fully that you run out of money.*
> —*Jonathan Clements*

Although these exceptions permit you to withdraw funds from your traditional IRA without penalty, remember that the funds withdrawn must be added to your other taxable income that year, and therefore will be fully taxable. The rules also require you to start taking withdrawals from your IRA plan by age seventy and a half.

### Roth Individual Retirement Accounts (Roth IRAs)

Any American who is planning seriously for financial independence needs to research the tax advantages of a Roth IRA. A Roth IRA differs from a regular IRA in that it does not allow you to deduct the money you contribute from this year's income for tax purposes. However, a Roth IRA does allow you to deposit up to $4,000 (in 2005) in a tax-sheltered fund where these funds will accumulate free of annual taxes until you retire, and then you can withdraw the accumulated funds tax free. The freedom from annual taxation on your growing mutual funds within your tax-sheltered Roth IRA allows your retirement fund to grow at a much greater accelerated rate than if your funds were subject to income taxes annually.

For example, if a thirty-five-year-old were to invest $4,000 every year for the next thirty years within a tax-sheltered Roth IRA and achieved a 10 percent growth annually, he would accumulate $798,931 by age sixty-five.

*Diversify Your Retirement Investments*

Consider placing each year's new pension deposit in a separate investment vehicle to maximize your flexibility. For example, if you need emergency funds in the future, you could collapse only one individual year's pension deposit of $10,000 or so rather than collapsing your complete fund. This would allow you to pay income tax on only the $10,000 you withdrew. After age fifty-nine and a half you can access your account under certain conditions that you should explore with a professional financial planner. Another advantage of depositing your pension in separate investment vehicles is that if you choose to take a year's sabbatical from earning a salary, you could withdraw some of your tax-sheltered pension funds to provide an income while you relax, study, or possibly volunteer for an extended missions trip. Although the withdrawn funds will be taxable, if you are not earning significant additional income that year, the tax burden generated by withdrawing funds that have been previously tax sheltered will be relatively light.

When you retire, you cannot know how long you will live. If you fear your investments will not provide you with an adequate income throughout your retirement years, you will be forced to live very conservatively using only the annual income generated by your investments plus your Social Security pension and your company pension (if you have one).

However, if you are forced to use the annual interest income and also to dip into the accumulated principal to generate a larger monthly retirement income, you may exhaust your invested funds before you and your spouse die. This is why I strongly suggest that you consider a reverse mortgage, using the equity in your home to enhance the monthly income from your pension. A wise retirement income plan that uses Social Security, any corporate pension, and your own investment income (possibly including a reverse mortgage) should provide the money you and your spouse need during your golden years.

## RETIREMENT-PLANNING WORKSHEET

How much monthly income will you need during your retirement? And to achieve that level of income, how much do you need to accumulate in investments to supplement your Social Security and company pension plan income? This worksheet will help you answer those questions.

To evaluate your retirement planning, answer the following questions:

1. Do you have a retirement investment program? _____

2. In what year do you plan to retire? _____

3. What amount of living expenses will you need to meet? (Consider mortgage or rental costs, property taxes, utilities, automobile costs, groceries, etc.) _____

4. How much monthly income do you want to receive to enjoy a comfortable retirement? _____

5. How much monthly income will Social Security provide?

_____

6. How much monthly income will be provided by your company's pension plan? _____

7. What is the shortfall between your monthly income goal and the amount Social Security and your company's pension plan will provide? _____

8. The amount you filled in as the answer to question 7 is the monthly amount of income you will need to generate from investments that you accumulate prior to retirement. Use the following table to determine what level of investments you will need to accumulate.

| Additional Monthly Income Needed | Amount of Capital Needed to Provide Additional Pension Income | | | |
|---|---|---|---|---|
| | Assumed Net Interest Rate After Tax on Your Retirement Fund | | | |
| | 5% Return | 6% Return | 7% Return | 8% Return |
| $1,000 | $240,000 | $200,000 | $171,428 | $150,000 |
| $2,000 | $480,000 | $400,000 | $342,856 | $300,000 |
| $3,000 | $720,000 | $600,000 | $514,284 | $450,000 |
| $4,000 | $960,000 | $800,000 | $685,712 | $600,000 |
| $5,000 | $1,200,000 | $1,000,000 | $857,140 | $750,000 |

# Chapter 13

# Tax Planning

## *How to Benefit from Tax Shelters*

*The only difference between a taxman and a taxi-
dermist is that the taxidermist leaves the skin.*

—Mark Twain

There are rumors that a new, simplified tax form is being developed to replace the cumbersome Form 1040. The proposed tax form would have only three lines:

A. How much did you earn last year?

B. What did you spend?

C. Send the government everything that's left.

You might think that joke is funny, but there is nothing humorous about the amount of our income that is consumed by various taxes. When you add up the taxes collected by all levels of government—local, state, and federal—it usually amounts to more than 45 percent of the money we earn. Most taxpayers work from January until May each year before beginning to earn a single dollar to spend for themselves and their families! Plus many studies reveal that the average taxpayer unintentionally overpays on his or her income taxes. No wonder. The IRS tax code for 2004 contains the equivalent of sixteen thousand pages of regulations plus an additional ninety-three thousand pages of explanations.

If you plan your finances carefully and obtain the best available tax advice, you can probably save thousands of dollars every year on unnecessary taxes. The tax codes are so complicated that very few citizens can utilize all the legally available exemptions and deductions without obtaining professional tax advice. Competent tax planners or accountants earn their fee several times over by gaining significant tax savings for their clients.

## BASIC TAXATION STRATEGIES

Following are some basic strategies that you should seriously consider:

*Maintain good records.* You should keep all receipts and vouchers related to home-repair expenses, because they may be deductible later. You may sell your home as an investment property, and any vouchers and receipts will validate tax-deductible expenses that would affect your adjusted cost basis to minimize your capital-gains tax.

*Determine the advantages of leasing.* If you intend to keep a car more than two years, leasing is often to your advantage from a taxation standpoint. However, if you replace your car every year and a half or so, owning your car can be more advantageous. Your accountant will be able to advise you on the best choice based on the latest tax changes.

*Consider a home office.* If you operate your own business, it might be to your advantage to establish an office in your home. You may deduct part of the rent or part of the mortgage interest in addition to a portion of the utilities and equipment expense. You must keep proper receipts and document all of your business expenses. The space used as a home office must be used for business purposes.

*Pay off nondeductible loans.* It is to your advantage to pay off your nondeductible debt first and then borrow money to purchase tax-deductible items. For example, use money in your investment fund to prepay your nondeductible high-interest loans. Then borrow the necessary funds to invest in new investment vehicles. The interest cost on this new loan will be tax deductible because the loan is for investment purposes.

*Adjust your withholding.* You should never have more money than is required withheld from your paychecks for income-tax prepayment. Many employees choose a higher level of withholding as a form of forced savings so they will receive a tax refund each year. However, you

> *When the government establishes a tax code that essentially robs Peter to pay Paul, they can always depend on the political support of Paul.*
> *—George Bernard Shaw*

receive no interest on your voluntary tax prepayments and no tax benefit. Always hold on to your money as long as you can. If you normally receive a significant income-tax refund, you are giving the government an unnecessary interest-free loan of your money.

*Don't prepay too little.* If you are an employee and also have your own side business, and if you expect to owe the IRS more than $1,000 in addition to the amount withheld from your paychecks, you are required to make quarterly estimated payments to the IRS. If you don't make such payments in a timely manner, the IRS will charge you a penalty, plus interest sometimes, plus the additional amount of tax that is owed.

*Take advantage of tax-sheltered savings.* Make the maximum deposit allowed by the IRS to your tax-deferred retirement savings plans (IRAs, for example) for yourself and your spouse as an essential part of your plan for financial independence.

*Benefit from depreciation.* Buy depreciating assets later in the year to maximize the tax write-off. For instance, self-employed people should buy their cars and major office equipment in December.

*Use all legitimate deductions.* Claim all proper tax deductions for investment purposes, including brokerage fees, safety-deposit box rental charges, and so forth.

Since tax rules and regulations change constantly, do not employ any of these strategies without first evaluating each one carefully with your tax counselor, lawyer, accountant, or professional financial planner.

Part 5

# PLANNING FOR THE FUTURE

# Chapter 14

# Finding Your
# Financial Balance

*How to Stop Worrying About Money*

*Work as if you were to live a hundred years,*
*pray as if you were to die tomorrow.*
—BENJAMIN FRANKLIN

A fter you have prudently done all you can to build and protect your
financial assets for your family, you need to do one last thing: place
all of it in God's hands and trust Him.

Remember, you are not embarking on this journey toward financial
freedom alone. God has provided numerous sound biblical principles that
will direct you toward financial independence. The Lord wants you to
escape the financial bondage that afflicts so many people in our generation:
"Beloved, I wish above all things that thou mayest prosper and be in health,
even as thy soul prospereth" (3 John 2). Jesus Christ wants you to achieve
prosperity in your spiritual life, your financial life, and your physical life
and health. He wants you to enjoy life and to be a significant blessing to
those around you.

## THE NEED FOR BALANCE IN YOUR FINANCES

It is important to maintain a balanced perspective by realizing that all of our financial concerns are only temporary. Although economic issues are important today and God commands us to act with diligence, all of this will someday pass away. Our ultimate spiritual destiny as Christians is to enter the heavenly city of God, the eternal New Jerusalem. The only key to heaven is our faith and trust in the salvation that Jesus Christ won for us by His sacrifice on the Cross. While our individual salvation is based solely on the Blood of Christ that was shed for each of us, all Christians will be judged at the Judgment Seat of Christ regarding their faithfulness to His commands. Those who have been faithful will receive crowns and mansions that they will enjoy forever.

One of the greatest tragedies of human nature is our tendency to postpone our enjoyment of the happiness that is available to us today in anticipation of a future happiness that will supposedly occur when we achieve some distant goal. That is a myth. Either we will choose to enjoy happiness and contentment today while on the journey, or we will miss out on one of the joys that God provides: the joy of progressively achieving our life goals. If we postpone our joy until we achieve that final goal, we will likely discover that the final goal will taste of ashes.

When the final spiritual accounting of our life is made before the Throne of God, our finances, our material possessions, and our achievements will count for nothing. The only items that will matter are the souls we have won to our Lord, the faithful and obedient service we have rendered to Jesus Christ, and the righteous deeds we have done for our brothers and sisters. Deeds of righteousness done for the love of Jesus Christ will be the true treasures that will count for eternity. Christ commanded us, "Lay up for yourselves treasures in heaven, where neither moth nor rust doth corrupt, and where thieves do not break through nor steal: For where your treasure is, there will your heart be also" (Matthew 6:20–21).

## OUR THANKFULNESS FOR GOD'S BLESSINGS

It is vital that we recognize and express our daily appreciation to God for the overwhelming blessings He provides to us. Anyone who seriously considers the opportunities and financial resources available to North American and European Christians in comparison to the billions who live in less-developed, less-prosperous countries will acknowledge that we are blessed. When we consider our blessings compared to virtually all those who lived in past centuries, we must acknowledge that we are truly blessed to live in this era. Our access to healthcare, medicine, sanitation, clean water, and economic opportunities are unmatched in past centuries and in most parts of the world today. The Word of God affirms that it is God's blessing that provides the gift of wealth: "But thou shalt remember the LORD thy God: for it is he that giveth thee power to get wealth, that he may establish his covenant which he sware unto thy fathers, as it is this day" (Deuteronomy 8:18).

As we consider our many blessings, we need to pause and appreciate what God has given us. We need to daily count our blessings and express our thanksgiving to our heavenly Father.

### The Role of Prayer

The role of prayer cannot be overemphasized. With our limited knowledge of our future, we often do not know exactly what we should do or what we should pray for. However, our Lord has provided for our need. He commands us to pray for wisdom so we will know what we should ask God to provide. James adds, "If any of you lack wisdom, let him ask of God, that giveth to all men liberally, and upbraideth not; and it shall be given him. But let him ask in faith, nothing wavering. For he that wavereth is like a wave of the sea driven with the wind and tossed" (James 1:5–6).

When we pray in faith for God to grant us wisdom, we can count on His promise that He will answer our prayer. With God's promised wisdom and the numerous biblical financial principles found throughout the Word of God, as illustrated in this book, we can confidently embark on our journey toward the financial freedom that will unlock God's blessings and His opportunities for us to bless others.

## Your Road to Financial Freedom

First, you must make the mental and spiritual commitment to change your previous unhealthy financial behavior and embark on the road to financial freedom. Next, it is important to study the principles outlined in this book and commit to developing new, successful habits. You need to review your current economic situation—assets, debts, and net worth—by completing the financial balance sheet at the end of chapter 2. Then begin the difficult but essential job of setting up a budget and paying off your debts to free yourself to build up your savings.

The key strategy is to take control of your money by paying your tithe to God and putting 10 percent of your monthly income into a savings account. Pay God and pay yourself first out of your paycheck; then pay everyone else. Once your savings grow to $5,000 and beyond, you can start methodically building your investments every month. As you seriously study the various investment choices, you will be able to choose the ones that are most appropriate to the level of risk you feel comfortable with. In addition, you should review the legal and financial tools available to protect your family's wealth: wills, a power of attorney, living trusts, and insurance policies.

You and your family can achieve financial freedom if you are committed to making these key changes in your behavior that will enable you to utilize your income through compound interest and wise investments.

As you begin your journey toward financial independence, you will be encouraged that you are now working to achieve your goals, not just to pay your bills. This freedom will transform your life. You will find that you can choose options that previously were not available to you: taking a sabbatical to relax, to study a subject you have always dreamed of, to volunteer with a ministry, or even to begin a new career. Many of those who achieve financial freedom take early retirement to explore new long-term possibilities in life—including the option to volunteer at or to work for a church, a charity, or a mission agency. What would you choose to do with the rest of your life if your money was working for you rather than you having to work for your money?

## FOLLOWING IN THE STEPS OF JESUS

Those who have placed their faith in Jesus Christ have made a commitment to follow in the steps of Jesus in every area of their lives. The Scriptures tell us that He has left "us an example, that ye should follow his steps" (1 Peter 2:21). How can we do this? Only through daily Bible study and prayer can we discern the path Christ wants us to follow to achieve a balanced and successful life.

Three times in the Bible we find the expression "like hinds' feet." In the book of Habakkuk we read, "The LORD God is my strength, and he will make my feet like hinds' feet, and he will make me to walk upon mine high places" (3:19). In a pastoral society, virtually everyone had witnessed shepherds caring for sheep and goats. Everyone knew that goats and sheep—like deer—were able to walk safely on ledges and other high places because their back feet track perfectly. As a goat walks on dangerous ledges, the animal can see only the careful placement of its front feet to avoid stones or a broken ledge; its rear hooves naturally follow in the exact places where the front feet previously stepped. Such an illustration tells us to place our spiritual feet perfectly in step behind Jesus, through the direction of His Holy Spirit.

God wants His disciples to follow the principles found in the Word of God to escape the spiritual and financial bondage that afflict so many in our society. He wants His followers to discover financial freedom that will enable us to assist our family, our church, and others around us who need help. My prayers are with you as you begin your lifelong journey toward financial freedom and independence. Achieving this will open up exciting new possibilities in your life.

After you have done all you can to build and protect your financial assets for your family, you need to do one last thing: place all of it in God's hands and trust Him. Jesus Christ told us, "Therefore take no thought, saying, What shall we eat? or, What shall we drink? or, Wherewithal shall we be clothed? (For after all these things do the Gentiles seek:) for your heavenly Father knoweth that ye have need of all these things. But seek ye first the kingdom of God, and his righteousness; and all these things shall be added unto you" (Matthew 6:31–33).

# APPENDIX

## Budgeting Worksheets

The following Web site is an excellent resource for worksheets you can use to monitor and calculate income and expenses. You can download the worksheets or work online. See www.todaysseniors.com/pages/Budget_Worksheets.html.

## Free Annual Credit Reports

The Fair Credit Reporting Act gives every American the right to obtain a free credit file from all three credit bureaus once each year.

Equifax Credit Information Services Inc.
P.O. Box 740241
Atlanta, GA 30374-0241
800-685-1111
www.equifax.com

Experian
888-397-3742
www.experian.com

TransUnion Corporation Consumer Disclosure Center
P.O. Box 2000
Chester, PA 19022
800-888-4213
www.transunion.com

*Financial Strength of Your Banks and Insurance Companies*

Consumers who want a detailed financial strength analysis of the banks, credit unions, savings and loans, and insurance companies they do business with can acquire this information from Weiss Ratings, Inc. or Veribanc. You can purchase Weiss reports at their Web site, www.WeissRatings.com, for $14.99 each, or by calling 800-289-9222 and paying $19.00 for each report. You can obtain Veribanc reports at www.veribanc.com at a cost of $10.00 for one bank rating and $5.00 for each additional rating.

*Ratings for Banks and Insurance Companies*

Look for a rating of A+ or better. You can find these ratings at:

- A.M. Best, 908-439-2200 or www.ambest.com
- Standard & Poor's, 212-438-1000 or www.standardandpoors.com

*Helpful Financial Web Sites*

- Calculating your insurance needs:
  www.finaid.org/calculators/lifeinsuranceneeds.phtml
- Planning for your retirement:
  www.calcbuilder.com/cgi-bin/calcs/RET2.cgi/usatoday
- Fraud information sources:
  www.usdoj.gov/criminal/fraud/Internet.htm

# Notes

## Introduction

1. "What Teens Don't Know about $$," *Parade,* June 27, 2004, 13.
2. "What Teens Don't Know," 13.
3. Thomas J. Stanley, *The Millionaire Mind* (Kansas City, MO: Andrews McMeel, 2000), 11.
4. Stanley, *The Millionaire Mind,* 173.

## Chapter 2: Building a Plan for Financial Freedom

1. U.S. Census Bureau, www.census.gov/PressRelease/www/releases/archives/income_wealth/002484.html (accessed November 2, 2004).
2. Steve Pavlina, "If No Shareware Professionals Are 100 Times Smarter Than You, Then Why Do Some Get 100 Times the Results? Part 1," Upload.it, http://upload.it/ita/upload_00003d.htm.
3. Pavlina, "If No Shareware Professionals."
4. Thomas J. Stanley, *The Millionaire Mind* (Kansas City, MO: Andrews McMeel, 2000), 3–4.
5. "Quotations by Winston Churchill," Word Power, www.word power.ws/quotations-churchill.html.

## Chapter 3: The Importance of Tithing and Charitable Giving

1. Cited in R. C. Sproul, "Financing the Kingdom of God," New Life Community Church, www.new-life.net/tithe2.htm.
2. Independent Sector, "Giving and Volunteering in the United States in 2001," www.independentsector.org/programs/research/gv01main.html.

*Chapter 4: Setting Up Your Budget*

1. John Maxwell, quoted in, Beth Skarupa, "Parents' Top Ten Money Mistakes: The Most Common Financial Errors and How to Avoid Them," iParenting.com, http://iparenting.com/resources/articles/moneymistakes.htm.

*Chapter 5: The Use and Abuse of Credit*

1. The Fair Credit Reporting Act gives every American the right to obtain a free credit file from all three major credit bureaus once each year.
2. Example of mortgage interest rates as of January 24, 2005, myFICO, www.myfico.com/myfico/CreditCentral/LoanRates.asp.
3. William Bonner and Addison Wiggin, *Financial Reckoning Day* (Hoboken, NJ: John Wiley & Sons, 2003), 204.
4. CardWeb.com, "Card Debt," www.cardweb.com/cardtrak/pastissues/may2004.html.
5. "Hooked on Credit," *Charlotte (NC) Observer,* December 7, 2004.
6. Michael T. Killian, "The Monthly Payment Scam," *Your Guide to Credit/Debt Management,* About, Inc., http://credit.about.com/cs/consumerwisdom/a/050197_2.htm.
7. Ted Wooley, *Fresh Start: The Authoritative Guide to Consumer Credit Repair,* quoted on ConsumerCreditRepair.com, www.consumer creditrepair.com/product.asp_Q_Txt_E_EXCERPTS_A_Item_E_1013W_A_xID_E_5.
8. efmoody.com, "Disability Probability," www.efmoody.com/insurance/disabilitystatistics.html.
9. Cited in Dave Ramsey, "The Truth About Debt," DaveRamsey.com, http://debt.daveramsey.com/etc/cms/debt/debt.html.
10. For more on this, see Dave Ramsey, *The Total Money Makeover* (Nashville, TN: Thomas Nelson, 2003).

*Chapter 6: Getting Smart About Homeownership and Mortgages*

1.  Michael T. Killian, "How Much Is a 'Ton of Interest'?" *Your Guide to Credit/Debt Management,* About, Inc., http://credit.about.com/cs/loansmortgage/a/02297.htm.

2.  Moshe Arye Milevsky, *Mortgage Financing: Floating Your Way to Prosperity* (Toronto, ON: York University, 2001), 10.

3.  Milevsky, *Mortgage Financing,* 2.


*Chapter 7: Investments Will Build Your Future*

1.  Cited in Tim Whitehead, "How to Tell Rover It's Over," Money Sense.ca, www.moneysense.ca/investing/stocks_markets/columnist.jsp?content=718172.

2.  Terrance Odean, "Terrance Odean's Investing Rules," Global Investor, http://books.global-investor.com/pages/gurus.htm?Mode=Rules&PerIndex=4307&ginPtrCode=00000&identifier=2b1128eb db684887bcfa1393071507cc.

3.  Cited in Jack Kemp, "The Greenspan Recession," Townhall.com, www.townhall.com/columnists/jackkemp/jk20010815.shtml.

4.  Alan Greenspan, *The Objectivist,* 1966, quoted in Ayn Rand, *Capitalism: The Unknown Ideal* (New York: Penguin, 1967).


*Chapter 8: Protect Yourself Against Fraud*

1.  Ryan Naraine, "B2C Goes from Rags to Riches," IT Service Management, http://itmanagement.earthweb.com/ecom/article.php/2196821.

2.  National Fraud Information Center, "Internet Fraud Statistics Reports," January-June 2004, www.fraud.org/janjune2004ifw.htm.

3.  Leonard Jacobs, "Survey: Charitable Giving Grows in 2003," BackStage.com, www.backstage.com/backstage/features/article_display.jsp?vnu_content_id=1000562254.

### Chapter 9: Insuring Against Financial Disaster

1. Life Insurance Management Association study, 1971.
2. *Journal of AMN Society of C.L.U.* 8, no. 1.
3. efmoody.com, "Disability Probability," www.efmoody.com/ insurance/disabilitystatistics.html.
4. Insurance Information Institute, "How Can I Save Money?" www.iii.org/individuals/homei/hbs/save/.
5. Rodney Vansil, "Protect What You've Worked For," *Owensville (KY) Messenger-Inquirer,* May 22, 2004, http://messenger-inquirer .com/specialpublications/EstatePlanning04/05_05-22-04.pdf.
6. Avolites Online, "Insurance Claim Form Gaffes," www.avolites .org.uk/jokes/insurance.htm.

### Chapter 12: Plan Now for a Successful Retirement

1. Rutgers University, "Retirement Facts and Figures," www.rce.rutgers .edu/money2000/pressroom/release.asp?id=3.
2. National Council on the Aging, quoted in "10 Key Financial Principles," Lemoyne Baptist Church, www.lemoynebaptist .org/financial.htm.
3. Stuart Foxman, "Retirement Cash: Will You Have Enough?" *Reader's Digest,* December 2003, 59–65.
4. Foxman, "Retirement Cash," 65.
5. Foxman, "Retirement Cash," 65.
6. Employee Benefit Research Institute, "The 1999 Retirement Confidence Survey Summary of Findings," www.ebri.org/rcs/1999/ rcssummary.pdf.
7. db65.com, "Retirement Facts," www.db65.com/retirementfacts .html.
8. Based on actuarial studies from life insurance companies.

9. William Bonner and Addison Wiggin, *Financial Reckoning Day* (Hoboken, NJ: John Wiley & Sons, Inc., 2003), 195.

10. Bonner and Wiggin, *Financial Reckoning Day,* 214.

11. Bonner and Wiggin, *Financial Reckoning Day,* 214.

12. Alan Greenspan, "Global Demographic Change: Economic Impact and Policy Challenges," a speech delivered February 28, 2004, quoted in Michael McKee and Craig Torres, "Greenspan Hits Alarm over Retiring Boomers," *National Post,* August 28, 2004.

13. McKee and Torres, "Greenspan Hits Alarm."

14. "Fast Facts and Figures About Social Security," published by the Social Security Administration, 2001 (June 2003 revision).